ESSENTIAL
AIRLINE SERVICE
ENGLISH

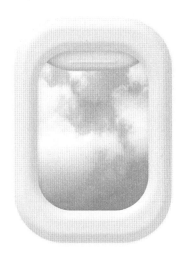

PREFACE

글로벌 세계경제 속에서 가장 비약적인 발전을 거듭하고 있는 항공서비스는 광범위한 지식과 기술 집약체 산업으로서 그 중요성이 더욱 강조되고 있다.

이 책은 항공서비스에 관한 수준 높은 서비스와 능숙한 현장업무 수행을 위해 필요한 내용을 제공하는데 도움을 주기 위한 목적으로 집필되었으며 일반 독자들에게도 전반적인 항공영어의 핵심적인 내용을 소개하고 있는 교재이다. 항공 및 관광 분야를 전공하는 학생들은 물론, 일선 항공업계 종사자들과 이 분야에 취업을 희망하거나 관심이 있는 일반 독자들에게 항공영어 전반에 관한 핵심적인 내용들이 업무흐름에 맞춰 집필되었다.

이 책의 체계는 크게 총 5장으로 구성되어 있다.

Unit 1. Check-In Service에서는 탑승예약에서부터 발권, 탑승수속을 다루고 있으며 Unit 2. Before Taking Off에서는 승객 탑승 안내와 좌석 배정, 기내 휴대 수하물 조치에 관련된 내용과 이륙 준비를 비롯하여 신문 서비스를 다루었다. Unit 3. En Route Service에서는 이어폰과 물수건 서비스, 식음료 서비스를 비롯하여 기내 음악과 영화 및 이어폰 관련 서비스와 기내 면세품 판매, 세관 및 입국신고서 그리고 검역 안내서와 관련된 내용 및 착륙과 승객 하기로 구성되어 있다. Unit 4. Walk Around and Personal Touch에서는 환자 서비스와 각종 편의 제공 서비스 및 고객 동향 파악, 목적지 도시 안내 및 입국심사와 세관안내를 다루고 있다. 마지막으로 Unit 5. Airline Announcements으로 구성되어 있다.

마지막 5장을 제외한 각 장은 대화문으로 구성하고 있으며 유용한 Tip과 다양한 참고자료를 통해 교재의 이해를 돕고 각 Unit의 학습한 내용을 Review Test로 정리할 수 있도록 하였다.

부족한 점은 추후 보완·발전시켜 나갈 것을 약속하며 본 저서가 산업체에서의 현장적응력을 높이는데 실질적인 도움이 되기를 바란다.

마지막으로 이 책이 출판되기까지 많은 분들의 노고와 격려가 있었기에 이분들께 머리 숙여 감사를 드린다. 이 책의 출판에 도움을 주신 임순재 사장님과 책의 완성을 위해 노력해 주신 편집부 직원 여러분에게도 진심으로 감사를 드린다.

2016년
저자 일동

CONTENTS

Unit 1 **Check-In Service** 항공예약 및 탑승수속

1. From Receiving to Confirming Reservations(탑승예약) … 2

    1) Receiving Reservations(예약접수) ··· 3

    2) Changing Schedules(예약변경) ·· 5

    3) Canceling Reservations(예약취소) ·· 6

    4) Confirmation(예약확인) ··· 6

2. About Ticketing(발권) … 8

3. Check-In(탑승수속) … 11

Unit 2 **Before Taking Off** 항공기 이륙 전

1. Boarding(승객 탑승 안내) … 20

    1) At the Boarding Station(탑승 시 안내 위치) ··· 21

    2) Zone Attendant(담당 승무원) ··· 23

    3) Passenger Request during Boarding(탑승 중 승객의 음료수 요구) ····················· 23

    4) Passenger with Heavy Bags(무거운 짐을 가지고 탑승한 승객 안내) ··················· 24

    5) Lavatory Use before Take-Off(이륙 전 화장실 사용) ··································· 26

    6) Mother with Infant(유아 동반 승객) ··· 27

    7) Young Child(어린이 승객 응대) ··· 28

2. Seating Arrangement(좌석 배정) … 29

    1) Separated Passengers(일행과 떨어진 좌석을 배정받은 승객에 대한 조치) ············· 30

2) No Empty Seats Available(빈 좌석이 없는 경우의 조치) ──────── 30

3) Wrong Seat(잘못된 좌석에 앉은 승객에 대한 조치) ──────── 32

4) Double Seating(중복 좌석에 대한 조치) ──────── 33

5) Changing Seats(좌석 변경 요청에 대한 조치) ──────── 33

3. Hand-Carry Baggage(기내 휴대 수하물) ··· 35

1) Baggage in the Aisle(통로 위 수하물에 대한 조치) ──────── 35

2) Baggage in the Overhead Bin(선반 위 수하물에 대한 조치) ──────── 36

3) Handling Baggage and Coats(기내 휴대 수하물과 코트) ──────── 37

4. Pre-Flight Check for Take-Off(이륙 준비) ··· 38

1) Seat Belt(안전벨트) ──────── 39

2) Tray Table and Seat Back(테이블과 좌석 등받이 원위치) ──────── 40

5. Newspaper Service(신문 서비스) ··· 43

Unit
3 En Route Service 비행 중의 서비스

1. Earphone and Towel Service(이어폰과 물수건 서비스) ··· 50

1) Earphone Service(이어폰 서비스) ──────── 51

2) Towel Service(물수건 서비스) ──────── 52

3) Movie Information Request(영화 정보 요청) ──────── 53

4) Movie Time Information(영화 상영 시간 정보) ──────── 53

2. Meal and Beverage Services(식음료 서비스) ··· 55

1) Beverage Service(음료 서비스) ──────── 56

2) Meal Service(식사 서비스) ──────── 61

3. In-Flight Music and Movie(기내 음악과 영화) ··· 76

4. Earphone Set Problems(이어폰 관련 문제) ··· 77

   1) Out of Order / Seat Available(시스템 고장 / 좌석 이동) ──────── 77

   2) Out of Order / No Empty Seats Available(시스템 고장 / 좌석이동 불가능) ─────── 78

   3) Bulkhead Passenger at Movie Time(스크린 앞쪽 승객) ──────── 80

5. In-Flight Sales(기내 면세품 판매) ··· 81

   1) General(면세품 판매 상황) ──────────────── 82

   2) Sales Items Request(면세품 주문) ──────────── 84

   3) In-Flight Sales(면세품 판매) ───────────── 86

6. Customs, Immigration and Quarantine(세관, 입국 및 검역 안내서) ··· 95

   1) Disembarkation Card / Tourist(입국신고서 / 관광객) ──────── 96

   2) Embarkation & Disembarkation Card / Transit Passengers(출국, 입국 신고서 / 통과 승객) ·· 96

   3) Transit without Visa(무사증 통과) ───────────── 97

   4) Customs Declaration Card / Resident and Tourist(세관신고서 / 거주자와 관광객) ─────── 98

   5) Customs Declaration Card / Passenger Given the Wrong Version Card

      (세관신고서 / 승객에게 잘못된 언어의 신고서 제공) ──────── 98

   6) Entering the United States of America(미국 입국) ───────── 103

7. Landing and Deplaning(착륙과 승객 하기) ··· 107

   1) Earphone Set Collection(이어폰 회수) ──────────── 108

   2) Seat Belt / Tray Table / Seat Back Situations(안전벨트 / 테이블 / 좌석등받이 위치) ·· 108

   3) Passenger in the Aisle Prior to Landing(착륙을 위해 통로에 있는 승객의 착석 유도) ·· 109

   4) Baggage Problems(승객 수하물 보관) ───────────── 110

   5) Collecting Cups(컵 회수) ──────────────── 110

   6) Deplaning and Farewell(하기와 작별) ──────────── 111

Walk Around and Personal Touch 고객동향 파악 및 맞춤 서비스

1. Handling Sick Passengers(환자 서비스) ··· 122

　1) Sick Passenger(환자) ──────────────────── 122

　2) Airsickness During the Flight(비행기 멀미 승객) ──────── 124

　3) Sore Throat(인후염) ──────────────────── 125

　4) Headache(두통) ──────────────────── 126

2. Service and Comfort(서비스와 각종 편의 제공) ··· 127

　1) Passenger Service Unit / Inexperienced Passenger

　　(승객 편의시설 / 비행기 시설에 익숙하지 않은 승객) ──────── 127

　2) Passenger Seat / Mechanical Instruction(좌석 작동설명) ──── 129

　3) Cabin Service(기내 서비스) ──────────────── 130

　4) Bored Passenger(지루한 승객) ──────────────── 132

3. Walking-Around Service(고객동향 파악) ··· 136

4. Destination City Information(목적지 도시 안내) ··· 142

　1) Transportation from the Airport to the Destination(공항에서 목적지까지의 교통수단) ·· 142

　2) Shopping Information(쇼핑정보) ──────────────── 143

　3) Hotel Information(호텔정보) ──────────────── 144

　4) Money Exchange Information(환전정보) ──────────── 145

5. From Immigration To Customs(입국심사, 세관 안내) ··· 146

　1) Immigration(입국심사) ──────────────────── 146

　2) Baggage(수하물) ──────────────────── 147

　3) Customs(세관) ──────────────────── 149

Unit 05 In-Flight Announcements 기내 안내방송

1. Pre-Boarding Announcement(탑승전 안내방송) ··· 154

2. Departure Delayed(출발 지연 방송) ··· 155

3. Flight Cancelled(결항 안내방송) ··· 156

4. In-Flight Announcement(비행중 안내방송) ··· 157

■ 참고문헌 ··· 169

Essential

Airline Service English

Unit 01 Check-In Service 항공예약 및 탑승수속

1. From Receiving to Confirming Reservations(탑승예약)

항공기의 좌석은 항공사의 주된 상품으로 세계 어느 곳에 있든지 승객이 원하는 행선지 여정(flight itinerary)에 따라 예약 가능하다. 항공사의 직원은 승객에게 각종 필요사항 및 서비스를 사전에 안내하고, 제한된 좌석의 판매를 효율적으로 관리한다. 예약을 받는 직원은 예약을 받을 때에 여행 날짜, 시간, 좌석의 등급, 연락 받을 주소와 전화번호, 돌아오는 항공편을 반복하여 확인할 수 있도록 한다.

Words & Phrases

- make a reservation : (좌석/객실/티켓 등을) 예약하다
  = book, reserve
  cf make an appointment : (진료/상담 등을) 예약하다
- available : (사물) 이용가능한/구할 수 있는
  (사람) 시간적 여유가 있는, 만날 수 있는, 연락 가능한
  cf 명사를 수식할 경우에는 명사 뒤에 위치함
- leaving for : ~로 떠나는/향하는
  = heading for
  = bound for
  = going to
  = to ~ (~행)
  ex Flight 567 to Chicago(시카고행 567편)
- confirm : 확인하다. 확정하다
  confirmation 확인
- flight schedule : 비행 일정, 비행기 시간
- cancel : 취소하다
- flight number : 항공기 편명

1) Receiving Reservations(예약접수)

Dialogue ❶

A : Airline agent / **P** : Passenger

A : Asiana Airlines. Kim speaking. Can I help you?

P : Yes. I'd like to make a reservation to New York on Mar. 23rd, in the afternoon.

A : Which class would you like? Business or Economy class?

P : I'll take a seat in Economy class.

A : Yes, we have some seats available.

P : Good. I'll take it.

A : All right. May I have your name?

P : Jin Hee Lee.

A : All right. Your reservation has been made for Flight 777 leaving for New York on Mar. 23rd, 6 p.m. Can I have your phone number, please?

P : Sure. 02-345-8763.

A : Please plan to arrive at the airport at least one hour before the departure time.

P : Thanks.

A : Thank you for calling Asiana Airlines. Have a nice day.

Dialogue ❷

A : Airline agent / **P** : Passenger

A : Korean Air. Park speaking. What can I do for you?

P : Yes. I'd like to make a reservation to Las Vegas.

A : When would you like to fly, ma'am?

P : On Aug. 15th.

A : All right. We have one flight at 4 p.m.

P : Sounds good. I'll take it.

A : Which class would you like to travel, First, Business or Economy?

P : I'll take Business class.

A : All right. Would you like to reserve your return flight, too, ma'am?

P : Sure. I'd like to return on Aug. 30th.

A : Aug. 30th. Let me check. We have some seats available at 7 p.m.

P : No problem.

A : Your name and phone number, please?

P : Minhee Lee and my phone number is 567-9855.

A : All right, Ms. Lee. Your reservation has been made for Flight 353 leaving for Las Vegas on Aug. 15th, Monday at 4 p.m..

And your return reservation on Aug. 30th, Friday at 7 p.m. is confirmed.

Your reservation number is 458755.

P : Thank you.

A : Thank you for calling Korean Air and have a good day.

Notes

- I'd like to ~ : ~하고 싶습니다(I want to~ 보다 정중한 표현)
- May I have/ask your name? : 성함을 말씀해 주시겠습니까?
  = Your name, please ?
  (×) What's your name? (무례한 표현임)
- Thank you for ~ing/명사 : ~해주셔서 감사합니다
  cf I'm sorry to ~ : ~해서 죄송합니다
- What can I do for you? : 무엇을 도와드릴까요?
  = How can I help you?
- Would you like to + 동사원형 ? : ~하시겠습니까?
- Would you like + 명사 : ~를 드릴까요/드시겠습니까?
  ex Would you like something to drink?
  cf Would you like me to ~ : 제가 ~해드릴까요?
- Let me ~(동사원형) : ~하겠습니다
  ex Let me check. 확인해 보겠습니다

2) Changing Schedules(예약변경)

Dialogue ❶

A : Airline agent / P : Passenger

A : Asiana Airlines. Kim speaking. May I help you?

P : Yes. I'd like to change the flight schedule.

A : All right. Your name, please?

P : Janet Lee.

A : Ma'am your reservation is Flight 023 going to Seattle tomorrow night?

P : Yes, but I'd like to take a morning flight.

A : Let me check for you.
　　We have some seats available on the flight at 9:00 a.m.

P : Great. Book me for the 9:00 a.m. flight, please.

A : All right, ma'am. Your flight has been changed from 023 to 025 leaving JFK at 9 a.m. and arriving in Seattle at 4 p.m. Is there anything else I can help you with?

P : No, not anymore. Thanks a lot.

A : My pleasure, ma'am. Thank you for flying with Asiana Airlines.

Notes

- Flight 023 going to Seattle : Seattle로 가는 023편
  = Flight 023 to Seattle
- Book me for ~ : ~를 예약해 주십시오
- leaving JFK : JFK 공항을 출발하는
  cf leaving for JFK(JFK 공항으로 가는)

3) Canceling Reservations(예약취소)

Dialogue ❶

A : Airline agent / P : Passenger

A : United Airlines. May I help you?

P : Hi. I'd like to cancel my reservation. Going to Hong Kong on May 3rd.

A : Can I have your name, please?

P : Robert James.

A : All right. Your reservation has been canceled. Is there anything else I can do for you, sir?

P : Oh... That's it. Thanks.

A : You're welcome.

Notes

· Is there anything else I can do for you? : 더 도와드릴 일은 없습니까?
· That's it. : 괜찮습니다. 더는 없습니다. 바로 그것입니다.
  cf. That's it? : 그뿐입니까? 그게 다입니까?

4) Confirmation(예약확인)

Dialogue ❶

A : Airline agent / P : Passenger

A : Singapore Airlines. Can I help you?

P : Hi. I'd like to confirm my reservation.

A : Can I have your name and flight number, please?

P : Mary Park and the flight number is 567.

A : All right. Your reservation is confirmed for Flight 567 to Chicago on May 5th, at 10 a.m.

Dialogue ②

A : Airline agent / P : Passenger

A : Delta Airlines. What can I do for you?

P : I want to reconfirm my reservation.

A : Can I have your name, please?

P : Maria Jason.

A : Are you leaving for New York on Wed. at 2 p.m.?

P : Yes. That's right.

A : Just for a second, please. Your reservation is confirmed.

P : Thank you.

A : My pleasure. Thank you for calling Delta Airlines.

Notes

• Flight 567 to Chicago : Chicago행 567편
• reconfirm : 재확인하다.

2. About Ticketing(발권)

항공사의 발권 카운터 직원은 운송약관, 요금, 초과 수하물 요금 및 운항시간표 등에 관한 제반 지식을 잘 숙지하고 있어야 한다. 발권 시 담당 카운터의 직원은 지급수단, 승객 여권상의 성명, 승객의 여정(출발도시, 경유지 및 도착지, 항공사 코드, 예약 좌석 등급, 운임 및 tax 기록 등)을 정확하게 확인하고 승객에게 항공권을 발급해야 한다.

Words & Phrases

- purchase : 구입/구매하다
  = buy
- reservation number : 예약번호
- round trip (ticket) : 왕복(티켓)
  one—way (ticket) : 편도(티켓)
- fare : 운임
  → 버스, 택시, 기차, 비행기, 선박 등 교통수단 이용요금은 모두 fare임
  비 fee(수수료), fine(벌금)
- Do you accept VISA? : 비자 카드도 됩니까?
- What class would you like? : 좌석등급은 어느 것으로 하시겠습니까?

Dialogue ❶

A : Airline agent / P : Passenger

A : Can I help you?

P : Yes. I'd like to purchase my ticket. My reservation number is JAL354.

A : All right. Can I have your name, please?

P : Yoo Mi Cho.

A : Japan Airlines to L.A. at 3 p.m.?

P : Right.

A : It's $900.00 for round-trip. How will you be paying?

P : Do you accept VISA?

A : Yes, we do.

P : Here it is.

A : Thank you, ma'am. Wait a second, please.

Thank you for waiting. May I have your signature here?

P : Sure. Here it is.

A : Thank you. Have a great day.

Dialogue ❷

A : Airline agent / P : Passenger

A : May I help you?

P : I'd like to purchase a ticket for Tokyo.

A : Did you make a reservation?

P : No, I didn't.

A : When would you like to fly?

P : Dec. 12th.

A : What class would you like?

P : Business class.

A : Would you like a round-trip ticket or one way ticket?

P : Round trip, please.

A : We have some seats available on the 5 p.m. flight.

P : That's good. I'll take it. How much is the fare?

A : It's $500.00 for round-trip.

P : Do you accept American Express?

A : Yes, we do. May I have your credit card, please?

P : Here it is.

A : Thank you. May I have your signature here?

P : Sure. Here it is.

A : Thank you very much.

Notes

· **How will you be paying?** : 결제는 어떻게 하시겠습니까?

　　will be ~ing(미래진행형), 여기서는 미래진행의 의미보다는 의사를 문의하는 정중한 표현

· **Here it is.** : 여기 있습니다.

　= Here you are

　= Here is your ~.

· **signature** : 서명

3. Check-In(탑승수속)

승객이 여권, 항공권 등을 제출하면 항공사의 직원은 제출한 서류의 예약여부를 확인하고 좌석을 배정해준다. 좌석배정 시 통로 측과 창가 측 중 승객의 선호좌석을 확인하고 좌석을 배정한다. 또한 수하물의 무게를 달아 이상유무와 좌석 등급별 수하물 허용량을 확인 후 수하물에 이상이 없을 경우 수하물표(baggage tag)를 부착하고 그 확인증(baggage claim tag)은 항공권에 붙여준다. 이 표는 도착지에서 수하물을 찾을 때나 수하물 분실시의 확인 여부를 위해 필요하다. 이러한 절차가 모두 끝나면 항공사 직원은 탑승권(boarding pass)에 명시된 탑승 구와 좌석번호, 항공기 번호를 다시 한번 승객에게 확인해준다.

Words & Phrases

- aisle : 통로
  - → 발음에 유의 aisle[ail]
- aisle seat : 통로측 좌석
  - ↔ window seat : 창측 좌석
- check : 수속하다. 부치다
  - EX Do you have any baggage to check?(부치실 가방이 있으십니까?)
- baggage claim check : 수하물 영수증
- boarding : 탑승
  - ↔ deplaning(하기)
  - boarding pass(탑승권)
  - boarding gate(탑승 게이트)
- emergency exit seat : 비상구 좌석
- carry-on = carry-on baggage(기내 휴대용 가방)

Dialogue ❶

A : Airline agent / P : Passenger

A : Good morning. May I help you?

P : Hi. (The passenger is putting their passport and ticket on the counter)

A : Which seat would you prefer, a window seat or an aisle seat?

P : Um... an aisle seat, please.

A : All right, ma'am. How many pieces of baggage would you like to check?

P : Just one. I'll carry this bag myself.

A : All right, ma'am.

Here's your boarding pass and baggage claim check. Boarding will begin at 4 p.m. The Gate number is 7.

P : All right. Thanks.

A : My pleasure, ma'am. Have a nice trip.

Dialogue ❷

A : Airline agent / P : Passenger

A : Let me see your ticket and passport, please.

P : Here you are.

A : Would you like an aisle seat or a window seat?

P : A window seat, please.

A : All right. Do you have any baggage to check?

P : Yes... two.

A : Would you put your baggage on the scale, please?

P : Sure.

A : Here are your boarding pass and baggage claim check.

Your seat is 10B on the aisle and the boarding Gate is 23. Boarding will begin at 2:40 p.m.

P : Thank you.

A : You're welcome. And enjoy your trip.

Dialogue ❸

A : Airline agent / P : Passenger

A : Good morning. Can I have your ticket and passport, please?

P : Here you are.

A : Would you like an aisle seat or a window seat?

P : Um... can I be assigned an emergency exit seat?

A : All right, ma'am but you may be asked to assist our crew members in the event of an emergency.

P : O.K. I see.

A : Do you have any baggage to check?

P : Yes... one.

A : Could you put your baggage on the scale, please?

P : All right.

A : Here are your boarding pass and baggage claim check.
Your seat is 23A and the boarding Gate is 30. Boarding will begin at 10 a.m.

P : Thank you so much.

A : You're welcome. Enjoy your trip.

Dialogue ❹

A : Airline agent / P : Passenger

A : Hello. Are you flying to St. Martin today?

P : Yes, I have my ticket here.

A : Great. I need to see your passport as well.

P : I have an e-ticket. Uh... is this the part you need?

A : Actually I just need your name and I can find you on the computer, sir.

P : Oh, O.K. It's Bates. Frank Bates.

A : Great. Here we are, sir.

P : Would I be able to get an aisle seat?

A : Certainly, sir.

P : Thanks.

A : Are you just checking these two bags today, sir?

P : Yes, I'll take my knapsack as my carry-on.

A : Did you pack these bags yourself?

P : Yes.

A : All right. Here is your boarding pass. Please be at the gate one hour prior to boarding time.

Notes

- I'll carry this bag myself. : 기내에 휴대할 가방입니다.
- Let me see ~ : ~를 보여주십시오.
  = May I see ~
- Would you like + 명사 : ~를 드릴까요/드시겠습니까?
  Would you like an aisle seat or window seat?
- scale : 저울
- assign : (좌석을) 배정하다
- be asked to ~ : ~하도록 요청받다
- assist : 조력하다. 돕다(=help)
- in the event of : ~의 경우에
- emergency : 비상. 응급상황
- Are you flying to St. Martin today? : 오늘 St. Martin으로 가십니까?
  → be + ~ing는 현재진행형(~하고 있다)이지만, 가까운 미래를 단정할 때도 쓰임.
- as well : 또한(=also). 마찬가지로
- knapsack : (작은) 배낭
- prior to : ~ 이전에(before)

● 출국절차

공항도착 → 탑승수속 → 수하물 위탁 및 좌석배정 → 출국장 입장 → 세관신고
→ 출국 보안검색 및 출국심사 → 탑승

● 입국절차

입국 서류 작성(기내) → 도착 → 입국심사 → 수하물 수취 및 세관검사

● 참고자료

1. 비상구열 좌석 배정안내

비상구열 좌석 배정 안내 Emergency Exit Row Seat Information

1. 손님이 배정 받으신 좌석은 비상구열 좌석입니다.
   You are assigned to an Emergency Exit Row Seat.

   좌석번호
   Seat No.

2. 만 15세 미만의 손님, 만 15세 미만의 어린이나 유아를 동반하신 손님, 글 또는
   그림의 형태로 제공된 비상 탈출에 관한 승객 브리핑 카드 (Safety Information Card)의
   내용을 이해하지 못하시는 손님은 비상구열 좌석 배정이 불가합니다.
   Passengers who are under the age of 15 or accompanying children under the age of 15,
   or passengers who cannot understand or perform the necessary actions during
   an emergency as shown on the Safety Information Card are prohibited from sitting in
   an Emergeny Exit Row Seat.

3. 비상구열의 좌석을 배정받으신 손님께서는 비상시 승무원의 지시에 따라 주시기
   바라며, 승무원의 지시없이는 절대로 비상구를 열어서는 안됩니다.
   Passengers seated in the Emergency Exit Row should follow the instruction of the cabin
   crew in the case of an emergency. (Passengers should not attempt to open the exit
   door without the crew's direction.)

▶ **American Culture 1**

자기소개(Introduction)

· 자기소개를 할 때 미국 사람들은 상대방과 눈을 맞춥니다. 우리나라에서 손윗사람을 대할 때 눈을 똑바로 쳐다보면 버릇 없는 사람이란 인상을 줄 수 있지만, 미국에서는 상대방의 눈을 피하면 부정적인 인상을 심어주게 됩니다.

· 처음 만난 사람들끼리 주로 악수(shake hands)를 하게 되는데 이때 2~3초간 굳게 잡습니다.

· 처음 만나서 하는 인사는 "Nice to meet you"라고 하고, 헤어질 때 인사는 "Nice meeting you"라고 합니다.

· 처음 만난 사이라면 상대방의 '성'(last name)을 불러주고 상대와 친근감이 생긴 후, 상대방의 동의 하에는 '이름'(first name)을 불러도 무방합니다.

· 그밖에 Mr. Mrs. Ms. Miss 등과 같이 성 (last name) 앞에 붙여 상대방을 존중함을 나타낼 수 있습니다.

☞ Mr.: Mister. Used as a courtesy title before the surname or full name of a man.

☞ Ms.: Used as a courtesy title before the surname or full name of a woman or girl

☞ Mrs.: Used as a courtesy title for a married or widowed woman before the surname or full name of her husband

☞ Miss: a title typically used for an unmarried woman

▶ **Grammar Note 1**: 허락을 요청할 때 쓰이는 표현법 Can, Could, May, Do you mind if~

1. Can, Could, May는 허락을 요청할 때 사용합니다. 여기서 Could는 Can의 과거 형태가 아님을 주의하세요.

예 · May I ask your name and room number, sir?

· May I come in to make up the room?

· Can I borrow your pen?

2. Do you mind if I ~는 상대방에게 불편을 주는 행동에 대한 허락을 요청할 때 사용합니다. (제가 ~해도 될까요?).

예 · Do you mind if I open the door? B: Yes, I do. It's very noisy outside.

· A: Do you mind if I smoke here? B: No, I don't.

주의 Do you mind if I ~의 경우 답변에 유의합니다. Not at all, No, I don't 와 같이 대답을 하면 그 의미는 허락을 한다는 의미입니다. 반면에, Yes, I do라고 대답한다면 허락을 할 수 없다는 의미입니다.

그 밖의 허락을 한다는 의미의 답변으로 사용될 수 있는 표현법으로는 Certainly not, Go ahead가 있습니다.

주의 비슷한 표현으로 Do you mind ~ing(~해주시겠습니까?)는 상대방에게 어떤 행동을 해달라고 요구할 때 사용합니다.

예 · Do you mind <u>turning</u> the volume down?

　(볼륨을 낮춰주시겠습니까?)

· Do you mind <u>fastening</u> your seat belt, please?

　(좌석벨트를 매주시겠습니까?)

주의 동사 Do 대신에 조동사 Would를 쓰면 보다 정중한 표현이 됩니다.

예 · Would you mind if I smoke here?

· Would you mind fastening your seat belt, please?

Review Test

1. Write the meaning of the following words.

   1) available _____

   2) departure _____

   3) reconfirm _____

   4) book _____

   5) purchase _____

   6) round-trip _____

   7) fare _____

   8) aisle _____

   9) boarding _____

   10) assign _____

   11) emergency _____

   12) knapsack _____

   13) carry-on _____

2. Complete the sentences with the correct words. Change the word form if necessary.

have	reservation	confirm	check
like	leaving	ask	leaving for

   1) Your reservation is made for Flight 353 _____ Las Vegas on Aug. 15th, Monday at 4 p.m.

   2) I'd like to _____ my reservation.

   3) Would you _____ a round-trip or one way ticket?

   4) How many pieces of baggage would you like to _____ ?

5) Can I _____ your name and flight number, please?

6) You may _____ to assist our crew members in the event of an emergency.

7) Your flight has been changed from 023 to 025 _____ JFK at 9 a.m. and arriving in Seattle at 4 p.m.

8) I'd like to make a _____ to New York on Mar. 23rd 6 p.m.

3. Fill in the blank(s) with suitable word(s).

1) I'd like to _____ a reservation to New York on March 23rd 6 p.m.

2) We have some seats _____ at 7 p.m.

3) Thank you _____ calling Asiana Airlines. Have a nice day.

4) Would you _____ _____ reserve your return flight, too?

5) Your reservation is Flight 023 _____ _____ Seattle tomorrow night?

6) Be at the gate one hour _____ _____ boarding time.

4. Translate the following into English.

1) 결제는 어떻게 하시겠습니까?

   _____.

2) 성함을 여쭤봐도 될까요?

   _____.

3) 더 도와드릴 일은 없습니까?

   _____.

4) 부치실 가방이 있으십니까?

   _____.

5) 볼륨을 좀 낮추어 주시겠습니까?

   _____.

Unit 02

Before Taking Off 항공기 이륙 전

1. Boarding(승객 탑승 안내)

　승객탑승은 일반적으로 출발 30분전부터 시작되며, 승무원들은 각자 정해진 위치에서 밝은 미소와 함께 명랑한 목소리로 탑승하는 승객에게 환영인사를 한다. 진심으로 환영한다는 느낌이 전달될 수 있도록 고객 한 분 한 분과의 인사가 제대로 이루어지도록 한다. 통로에서 승객과 마주칠 경우에는 미소와 함께 가벼운 목례로 인사를 한 뒤 한쪽으로 비켜선다. 탑승 구에서 환영인사를 하는 승무원은 탑승권에 기재된 목적지와 좌석번호를 확인하고 왼쪽(L side)와 오른쪽(R side)을 구분하여 안내한다. 객실 내에 위치한 승무원은 담당구역에서 원활한 승객 탑승 진행을 위해 이동하면서 보다 적극적인 안내를 실시한다. 특히 유아동반 승객이나 노약자, 환자, 장애인, 어린이 등 도움을 필요로 하는 승객에게는 보다 적극적으로 안내하도록 한다.

Words & Phrases

- Welcome aboard. : 탑승을 환영합니다(비행기, 선박 등)
- I'll get it for you. : 가져다 드리겠습니다
- I'm sorry to have kept you waiting. : 기다리시게 해서 죄송합니다
- Would you mind keeping your bags under the seat in front of you?(가방을 앞좌석 밑에 보관해 주시겠습니까?)
- take-off : 이륙
  ↔ landing (착륙)
- during the flight : 비행중
- boarding pass : 탑승권
- cabin : (선박, 항공기의) 객실
- as soon as possible : 가능한 한 빨리

1) At the Boarding Station(탑승 시 안내 위치)

Dialogue ❶

F : Flight attendant / **P** : Passenger

F : Good morning. Welcome aboard.

   May I see your boarding pass, please?

P : Yes... here you are. It's 23D.

F : Thank you. Your seat is in the back of the cabin on your right.

P : Thanks.

Dialogue ❷

F : Flight attendant / **P** : Passenger

F : Good afternoon. Welcome aboard.

   Can I see your boarding pass, please?

P : Sure. It's 45C.

F : Thank you. Please take the aisle to the left.

P : Thanks.

Dialogue ❸

F : Flight attendant / P : Passenger

P : Excuse me. Um... my seat is 14B. Where is it?

F : Please take the aisle to the right.

P : Thanks.

F : My pleasure.

Dialogue ❹

F : Flight attendant / P : Passenger

F : Good afternoon, ma'am. Welcome aboard.

P : Hello, Where is 10J?

F : Please take the other aisle.
　　Your seat is in the front of the cabin.

P : Thanks.

F : You're welcome, ma'am.

Notes

· Take the aisle to the left. : 왼쪽 통로로 가시면 됩니다
· the other aisle : 다른 쪽 통로
· in front of : ～앞

2) Zone Attendant(담당 승무원)

Dialogue ❶
F : Flight attendant / P : Passenger

F : May I have your boarding pass, please?

P : Yes... here you are.

F : Thank you. Your seat number is 52A. This way, please.

P : Thanks.

Dialogue ❷
F : Flight attendant / P : Passenger

F : Welcome aboard. May I see your boarding pass, please?

P : Yes... here it is.

F : Thank you. The aisle seat... right here.

P : Thanks.

3) Passenger Request during Boarding(탑승 중 승객의 음료수 요구)

Dialogue ❶
F : Flight attendant / P : Passenger

P : Excuse me. Can I have some water?

F : Certainly. I'll get it for you immediately.

   (After a while)

F : Here is your drink, sir.

P : Thanks.

F : My pleasure.

Dialogue ❷

F : Flight attendant / **P** : Passenger

P : Excuse me. I feel thirsty. Can I have some water?

F : Yes, but after everyone has boarded, I'll get it for you as soon as possible.

P : Thanks.

(After a while)

F : I'm sorry to have kept you waiting. Here is your drink.

P : Thanks.

F : You're welcome.

Notes

- immediately : 바로, 즉시
  = right away
  유 soon(곧, 금방), shortly(곧)
- thirsty : 갈증이 나는
- I'm sorry to ~ : ~해서 죄송합니다
  예 I'm sorry to have kept you waiting.(기다리시게 해서 죄송합니다.)

4) Passenger with Heavy Bags(무거운 짐을 가지고 탑승한 승객 안내)

Dialogue ❶

F : Flight attendant / **P** : Passenger

F : Good morning? May I help you with your bag?

P : Yes, please. Thanks.

F : My pleasure. May I help you find your seat?

P : Yes... it's 13B.

F : This way, please. Here is your seat. Have a nice flight.

Dialogue ❷

F : Flight attendant / P : Passenger

F : Good afternoon? May I help you with your bags?

P : Yes. Thanks.

F : You're welcome. Can I have your boarding pass, please?

P : Here you are.

F : This way, please. Here is your seat.

    Would you mind keeping your bags under the seat in front of you, please?

P : Sure. Thank you.

F : My pleasure. If you need any further assistance, please let us know.

Notes

- May I help you with your bag? : 가방 드는 걸/옮기는 걸 도와드릴까요?
- Would you mind : ~해주시겠습니까?(정중한 요청)
  = Do you mind ~ing?
  ex Would you mind keeping your bags under the seat in front of you?
- further : (형용사) 더 이상의, (부사) 더 이상

5) Lavatory Use before Take-Off(이륙 전 화장실 사용)

Dialogue ❶

F : Flight attendant / P : Passenger

P : Excuse me. May I use the lavatory now?

F : Would you mind using the lavatory after take-off, please? I'm sorry, ma'am.

P : That's O.K.

Dialogue ❷

F : Flight attendant / P : Passenger

P : Excuse me. Can I use the lavatory?

F : Would you mind using the lavatory after take-off, please?

P : But... I can't wait.

F : Well... All right. Please hurry. We'll be taking off shortly.

P : Thanks.

Notes

· lavatory : 화장실
· Would you mind using the lavatory after take-off? : 이륙한 후에 화장실을 이용해
주시겠습니까?
· shortly : 곧

6) Mother with Infant(유아 동반 승객)

Dialogue ❶

F : Flight attendant / **P** : Passenger

F : Good morning? May I help you with your bags?

P : Yes, please. Thanks.

F : You're welcome. Can I see your boarding pass, please?

P : Here you are.

F : This way, please. This is your seat.
Would you like a bassinet?

P : Yes, please.

F : I'll get one for you after take-off.
Would you please fasten your seatbelt only around yourself and hold your
baby outside the seatbelt?
It will be safer and more comfortable for the baby.

P : Thank you.

(After take-off, F/A is back with a bassinet to the passenger)

F : Would you like me to set up the bassinet for you?

P : Thank you.

F : We also have diapers, bottles, baby food and formula.
If you need anything during the flight, just let me know. Have a nice flight.

Notes

· bassinet : 요람, 아기침대
· diaper : 기저귀
· formula : 분유
· during the flight : 비행 도중
  during + 명사(~하는 동안)

7) Young Child(어린이 승객 응대)

Dialogue ❶

F : Flight attendant / **P** : Passenger

F : Hi. What's your name?

P : Soo min.

F : Soo min. That's beautiful name. And how old are you?

P : I'm six.

F : Oh, six years old? Do you want some toys to play with?

P : Yes.

F : Okay. I'll bring them for you.

P : Thank you.

(After a while)

F : Here you are. Be a good girl.

P : Thank you.

F : You're welcome.

Notes

· I'll bring them for you.
= I'll get it for you.

2. Seating Arrangement(좌석 배정)

좌석에 여유가 있는 경우에도 원칙적으로는 승객의 탑승권에 기입된 좌석에 따라 정확히 안내할 수 있도록 하고 모든 승객의 탑승 완료 후 승객의 별도 요구에 따라 조치를 취할 수 있도록 한다. 일행인 승객들은 가능한 함께 앉을 수 있도록 배려하고 승무원의 편의를 위해 승객이 좌석을 옮기길 무리하게 종용해서는 안 된다. 중복좌석(double seat)의 경우에는 먼저 양 승객에게 양해를 구한 뒤 사무장에게 보고 한 뒤 지상직원에 의해 좌석을 재배정 받을 수 있도록 조치한다. 가장 먼저 탑승권을 확인하여 승객의 이름과 좌석번호를 확인 후 나중에 탑승한 승객을 승무원 좌석(jump seat)에서 기다리도록 권유하고 사무장에게 보고한다. 사무장은 지상직원에게 좌석을 재배정 받고 좌석이 재배정 되면 승무원은 승객을 새로운 좌석으로 안내하고 좌석중복으로 불편을 끼친 점을 다시 한번 정중히 사과한다. 비상구 좌석에 착석한 승객들이 노약자, 어린이, 환자 등과 같이 부적합하지 않은지 확인하고 착석승객에게는 비상시의 행동요령에 대하여 안내한다.

Words & Phrases

- occupied : (좌석이) 다 찬
  ↔ empty (좌석이) 빈
- I'm afraid you're in the wrong seat. : 죄송하지만 좌석이 여기가 아닙니다.
- I'm sorry to bother you. : 방해해서 죄송합니다.
- I'm very sorry for the inconvenience. : 불편을 끼쳐드려 죄송합니다.
- arrange : 마련하다, 준비하다, 주선하다, 정돈하다
- assign : (좌석을)배정하다, 배치하다
- Is it possible that ~ : ~할 수 있습니까?
- I'll see if ~ : ~인지 확인해 보겠습니다.
- Would you care to ~ : ~하시겠습니까?
- Would that be alright? : 괜찮으시겠습니까?

1) Separated Passengers(일행과 떨어진 좌석을 배정받은 승객에 대한 조치)

Dialogue ❶

F : Flight attendant / **P** : Passenger

P : Excuse me. My friends are sitting over there, and we want to sit together.
  Is it possible that we can sit together?

F : I'll see if it can be arranged after take-off, sir.
  I'll be back soon and let you know.

P : O.K. Thanks.

  (After take-off)

F : Thank you for waiting. We have some seats available in the back of the cabin, sir.
  Would that be alright?

P : Yes, that would be fine.

F : This way, please.
  Here are your seats. Have a nice flight.

> **Notes**
>
> • over there : 저쪽에(↔ over here)
> • I'll see ~ : ~를 확인해 보겠습니다
> • arrange : 준비하다. 정리하다

2) No Empty Seats Available(빈 좌석이 없는 경우의 조치)

Dialogue ❶

F : Flight attendant / **P1** : Passenger 1 / **P2** : Passenger 2

P1: Excuse me. My wife and I were assigned separate seats.

F : Just a moment, please. I'll see if it can be arranged, sir.

P1: O.K. Thanks.

(After a while)

F : I'm sorry, sir, but I'm afraid all the seats are occupied. Where is your wife sitting?

P1: Over there. Across the aisle.

F : Let me check whether another passenger is willing to change his or her seat for you.
Just a moment, please.

(F/A approaches P2 for asking changing seats with couples seated separately.)

(To P2)

F : Excuse me. I'm sorry to bother you, but we have a couple who has been assigned separate seats. Would you care to change seats so they can sit together?

P2: No problem. Where should I sit?

F : Thank you very much. I will show you where it is. This way, please.

(To P1)

F : Sir, this lady is willing to change seats with you.

P1 : Thank you very much.

(To P2)

F : Ma'am, Here you are. Thank you indeed. I really appreciate it.

P2: My pleasure.

F : Have a nice flight.

- assign : (좌석을) 배정하다
- Would you care to ~ : ~하시겠습니까?
  = Would you like to ~
- so(=so that) they can sit together : 그들이 같이 앉을 수 있도록
- be willing to ~ : 기꺼이 ~해주다
- I really appreciate it. : 정말 감사드립니다

3) Wrong Seat(잘못된 좌석에 앉은 승객에 대한 조치)

Dialogue ❶

F : Flight attendant / P1 : Passenger 1 / P2 : Passenger 2

P1 : Excuse me. I think this is my seat but someone is in it.

F : May I see your boarding pass, please? Thank you.

(To P2)

F : Excuse me. May I see your boarding pass, please?
I'm afraid you're in the wrong seat. Your seat is behind this one.
Would you please change seats?

P2 : Oh... really? I'm sorry. Where is my seat?

F : This is your seat. Have a pleasant flight.

P2 : Thank you.

- I'm afraid (that) ~ : 죄송하지만......(정중한 표현)
  → I'm sorry, but ~과 거의 같은 의미로 쓰임
  ex I'm afraid not.(그렇지 않은 것 같다.)
  I'm afraid so.(그런 것 같다.)

4) Double Seating(중복 좌석에 대한 조치)

Dialogue ❶

F : Flight attendant / P : Passenger

P : Excuse me. Someone is in my seat.

F : Can I see your boarding pass, please?

　　I'm afraid that there has been a mistake in seating arrangements.

　　Would you mind waiting here, ma'am? I'll check it for you immediately.

P : Sure.

　　(After a while)

F : Thank you for waiting. Your seat has been rearranged. It's 56A.

　　May I assist you to your seat?

　　Here you are. I'm very sorry for the inconvenience.

　　Would you care for something to drink?

P : No, thanks. That's alright.

F : I am very sorry for the inconvenience. Have a nice flight.

Notes

> Would you care for + 명사 : ~를 드릴까요?/드시겠습니까?
> = Would you like + 명사
> Would you care for something to drink?

5) Changing Seats(좌석 변경 요청에 대한 조치)

Dialogue ❶

F : Flight attendant / P : Passenger

P : Excuse me. Do you have any empty seats in the front of the cabin?

F : I'm not sure, but I'll check and let you know after take-off.

P : O.K. Thanks.

(After take-off)

F : We have some empty seats in the middle of the cabin. Would that be alright?

P : Yes, that's fine.

F : This way, please. Here you are. Enjoy your flight.

Dialogue ❷

F : Flight attendant / P : Passenger

P : Excuse me. I'd like to change my seat.

F : Where would you like to sit, sir?

P : In the front and an aisle seat, please.

F : I'll see what's available.

(After a while)

F : Thank you for waiting. I'm sorry, but I'm afraid all the seats in the front are occupied.

P : Oh...... really? O.K.

F : I'm sorry, sir. If you need anything during the flight, please let me know.

P : O.K. Thanks.

Notes

· I'll check and let you know. : 확인 후 알려드리겠습니다.
· Would that be alright? : 괜찮으시겠습니까?

3. Hand-Carry Baggage(기내 휴대 수하물)

승객의 기내 반입 수하물 중 가벼운 물건은 머리 위 선반(overhead bin)에 보관하도록 하고 무거운 물건, 깨지기 쉬운 물건은 좌석 밑에 보관하도록 안내한다. 비상상황 시 승객의 원활한 탈출을 위해 문 쪽이나 통로 주변에 짐이 방치되지 않도록 한다. 승객의 재킷(jacket)이나 코트(coat) 등은 구겨지지 않게 잘 접어서 보관해드리도록 하고 옷장(closet)이 있는 경우에는 여권이나 지갑 등 중요 소지품을 승객이 직접 보관하게 안내한 다음 좌석 번호를 표시하고 보관한다. 좌석 밑이나 선반에 보관할 공간이 없는 경우 승객의 짐을 보관해드릴 때에는 보관장소를 말씀 드리고, 내용물을 확인하고 보관할 수 있도록 한다.

Words & Phrases

- keep the aisle clear : 통로를 비워두다.
- overhead bin : 선반
- Would you mind ~ing? : ~해주시겠습니까?
- Would you like me to ~? : 제가 ~해드릴까요?
- I'll keep it here. : 제가 가지고 있을게요.
- Enjoy the flight. : 즐거운 비행 되십시오.

1) Baggage in the Aisle(통로 위 수하물에 대한 조치)

Dialogue ❶

F : Flight attendant / **P** : Passenger

F : Excuse me. Is this bag yours?

P : Yes.

F : I'm sorry but we have to keep the aisle clear.

Would you mind keeping your bag under the seat in front of you, please?

P : Oh, sorry.

F : Thank you. Have a nice flight.

Dialogue ❷
F : Flight attendant / P : Passenger

P : Excuse me. My bag doesn't fit under the seat and the overhead bin is full.

F : Would you like me to keep your bag in the coatroom?

P : Would you do that? Thanks.

F : My pleasure. Have a nice flight.

Notes

- fit : 들어맞다
- Would you like me to ~ : 제가 ~해드릴까요?
  cf Would you like to ~(~하시겠습니까?)
- coatroom : 옷장

2) Baggage in the Overhead Bin(선반 위 수하물에 대한 조치)

A passenger with heavy bag

Dialogue ❶
F : Flight attendant / P : Passenger

F : Excuse me. Your bag is too heavy for the overhead bin.

Would you mind keeping your bag under the seat, please? It might fall out during the flight. Thank you. Have a nice flight.

· too heavy for ~ : ~에 (들어가기에는) 너무 무겁다
· might fall out : 떨어질 수도 있다, 떨어질지도 모른다

3) Handling Baggage and Coats(기내 휴대 수하물과 코트)

Dialogue ❶
F : Flight attendant / P : Passenger

F : Excuse me. Would you like me to hang your coat in the coatroom?

P : Yes, please. Thank you.

F : You're welcome. Have a nice flight.

Dialogue ❷
F : Flight attendant / P : Passenger

F : Excuse me. Would you like me to keep this bag for you in the back of the cabin?

P : Yes, thanks.

F : You're welcome. Have a nice flight.

Dialogue ❸
F : Flight attendant / P : Passenger

F : Excuse me. Would you like me to keep this for you in the coatroom?

P : No, thanks. I'll keep it here.

F : All right, sir. Enjoy the flight.

· I'll keep it here. : 제가 가지고 있을게요.

4. Pre-Flight Check for Take-Off(이륙 준비)

항공기 이륙 전 비행기가 활주로로 이동하게 되면 환영인사 방송과 함께 승무원들은 각자 자신의 담당구역에서 인사를 한다. 환영인사에 이어 승객들의 비상상황에 대한 안내 방송과 행동요령에 대한 시범이 이루어진다. 승무원들은 이륙 전에 승객의 안전사항을 확인하고 유동물질 고정 및 항공기내 시설물의 상태를 점검하고 승무원도 지정된 좌석(jump seat)에 착석해서 좌석벨트를 착용해야 한다. 이륙 전 승객안전에 관한 체크사항은 승객의 착석 및 좌석벨트의 착용여부, 좌석 등받이, 트레이 테이블(tray table), 팔걸이(arm rest)의 원위치 상태를 확인하고 승객의 휴대 수하물 및 유동물건의 고정여부, 문 쪽이나 통로의 청결 상태, 화장실 점검 및 승객의 사용여부, 비상구 주변 정리, 승객 선반의 닫힘 상태, 전자제품 사용 안내 및 확인 등이다. 특히 좌석벨트를 아기와 엄마가 함께 매고 있는 경우 좌석벨트 밖으로 엄마가 아기를 안도록 안내한다.

Words & Phrases

- Would you mind fastening your seat belt, please? : 좌석벨트를 매주시겠습니까?
- We'll be taking off shortly. : 곧 이륙하겠습니다.
- fold(=close) the tray table : 테이블을 접다
  - ↔ unfold/open the tray table
- seat back : 좌석 등받이
- reclined : 기울어진, 기대어진
  recline (동사) 기대다, 기울이다
- departure : 출발 ↔ arrival(도착)
- come on board : 탑승하다 = board
  - aboard (형용사) 탑승한

1) Seat Belt(안전벨트)

A passenger doesn't fasten his / her seat belt

F : Flight attendant / **P** : Passenger

Dialogue ❶

F : Excuse me. Would you mind fastening your seat belt, please?
We'll be taking off shortly. Thank you. Have a nice flight.

Child with loose belt

F : Flight attendant / **P** : Passenger

Dialogue ❷

F : Hi. Let me put a pillow under your seat belt.
That's better, isn't it?

OR

F : Would you like me to put this pillow under your seat belt?
It'll be more comfortable.

A passenger refuses to fasten the seat belt

F : Flight attendant / **P** : Passenger

Dialogue ❸

F : Excuse me. Would you mind fastening your seat belt, please?
We'll be taking off shortly. Thank you.

P : I don't like fastening the seat belt. Don't worry.

F : I'm sorry but I must ask you to fasten your seat belt for take-off. It's an airline regulation for your safety. After take-off, when the fasten seat belt sign is off, you can unfasten your seat belt. Thank you for you cooperation.

Notes

- shortly : 곧
  = soon
- comfortable : 편안한
- pillow : 베개
- refuse to ~ : ~하기를 거부하다
- ask + 사람 + to 부정사 : ~에게 ~해달라고 요청하다
- airline regulation : 항공 규정/규칙
- unfasten : 풀다
- cooperation : 협조, 협력

2) Tray Table and Seat Back(테이블과 좌석 등받이 원위치)

Tray table open

Dialogue ❶

F : Flight attendant / **P** : Passenger

F : Excuse me. Would you mind folding your tray table, please?
We'll be taking off soon. Thank you.

Seat back in reclined position

Dialogue ❷

F : Flight attendant / **P** : Passenger

F : Excuse me. Would you mind returning your seat back to the upright position, please?
We'll be taking off shortly. Thank you.

Delay in departure

Dialogue ❸

F : Flight attendant / **P** : Passenger

P : Excuse me. Why is there a delay?

F : I'm sorry, ma'am. We're waiting for a few more passengers to board. We'll be taking off as soon as they arrive.

- upright position : 똑바로선 위치/자세
- delay : 지연
- wait for + 사람 ~(to 부정사) : …가 ~하기를 기다리다
- as soon as : ~ 하자마자

● 참고자료

1. 안전여행 안내서

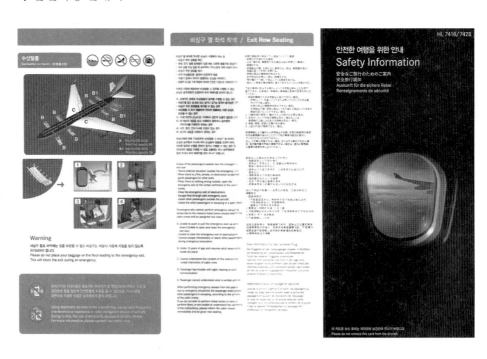

5. Newspaper Service(신문 서비스)

 승객의 탑승구 입구에 신문 카트(cart)를 준비하여 승객이 직접 선택하여 볼 수 있도록 서비스하고, 서비스 후에 남은 신문과 잡지는 매거진 랙(magazine rack)에 제호가 잘 보이도록 종류별로 꽂아 두거나 비행 중에 계속 서비스한다.

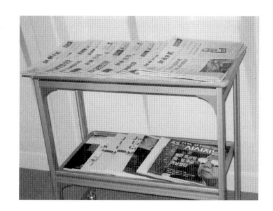

Words & Phrases

· The Time magazine is not available on this flight. : 금번 비행에는 타임지가 제공되지 않습니다.
· instead : 그 대신
  instead of + 명사(~대신에)
· on board : 기내에
  = on this flight
· Would you care for + 명사
  = Would you like + 명사(~를 드릴까요?)
· magazine rack : 잡지 비치함

Offer

Dialogue ❶
F : Flight attendant / P : Passenger

F : Would you like to read a newspaper?
    Here you are.

Run out of newspaper and magazine

Dialogue ❷

F : Flight attendant / **P** : Passenger

P : Can I have a TIME magazine?

F : I'm sorry but I'm afraid we have run out of TIME magazines.

OR

I'm sorry but the TIME is not available on this flight.

Dialogue ❸

F : Flight attendant / **P** : Passenger

P : Can I have a L.A. Times?

F : I'm sorry but I'm afraid we don't have the L.A. Times on board. Would you care for Korea Herald, instead?

P : Okay.

F : Here is your newspaper. Have a nice flight.

Notes

- run out of : 다 떨어지다. 바닥나다
- I'm sorry but I'm afraid ~ : 죄송하지만 ~인 것 같습니다
  → I'm afraid ~는 유감스러운 사실을 완곡하게 말할 때 쓰임

● 참고자료

1. 비상구 좌석 브리핑 안내문

EXIT SEATING

IF YOU ARE ASSIGNED AN EXIT ROW SEAT ....
You may be asked to assist our crew members in the event of an emergency.
You may be required to follow the directions of our crew members to perform the following tasks.
■Keep other passengers clear of the emergency exit door until crew members securely open it.
■After evacuating, assist other passengers coming down the emergency slide.
■Direct other passengers to evacuate away from the aircraft immediately.
■Others (Crew members will instruct the task when it is necessary.)
Please read the safety instructions leaflet in your seat pocket at your earliest convenience after boarding.   Thank you.
Japan Airlines. Japan Asia Airways. Japan TransOcean Air. Japan Air Charter. JAL EXPRESS. J-AIR.
Civil Aviation Bureau Ministry of Transport Japan
TS-41070

EMERGENCY EXIT SEAT BRIEFING SCRIPT(비상구 좌석 브리핑 안내문)

안내여부확인	Are you informed about Emergency Exit Seat?
비상구 좌석 개요 안내	* You're now seated on Emergency Exit Seat, and this is the emergency exit door. * Passenger in Emergency Exit Seat should help flight attendants(crew members) to evacuate passenger in case of emergency. * Do you agree? / Will you help us as I told you? / Will you help me in case of emergency?
승객의사에 따른 처리	〈승객이 협조 의사를 밝히는 경우〉 * Thank you, sir / ma'am. * Please read carefully this Safety Information Card. It explains exit seat exit responsibilities. If there is any question, please let me know. 〈승객이 협조를 거부하는 경우〉 * I see, sir / ma'am * In that case, we need to rearrange a passenger who is willing to help us because Aviation law states.

▶ Grammar 2: 요청할 때 쓰는 표현

1. can, will, could, would 는 누군가에게 무엇인가를 요청할 때 쓰이는 표현입니다. could 와 would 가 보다 공손한 표현입니다.

> 예 · Can you drop off the mail?
> · Will you pay the bill?
> · Could you open the window?
>
> 좀더 공손한 표현
>
> · Would you pick up the mail?

■ 긍정의 대답

> 예 · Would you sign the check, please? Of course. / Sure. / Certainly.

■ 부정의 대답: 거절에 대한 사과와 함께 거절의 이유를 설명해줍니다.

> 예 · Could you open the window? I'm sorry, I can't. It's cold in here.

주의 대답할 때 could 와 would 로 하지 않도록 주의 해야 합니다.

> 예 · Could you open the window? I'm sorry, I couldn't. (X)
> · Would you sign the check, please? Sure. I would. (X)

2. Would you like to 와 Like

■ Would like to + 동사원형: 상대방의 의사를 문의하는 정중한 표현입니다.
(~하시겠습니까?')

> 예 · Would you like to run a tab or pay cash?
> · Would you like to order?

■ I'd like to ~(= I would like to ~) : 본인의 의사를 정중히 표현할 때 사용합니다.
(~하고 싶습니다.)

■ Like 는 다른 동사를 함께 사용 할 때 중간에 'to'를 함께 써야 합니다. '~하기를 좋아하다' 뜻으로 해석됩니다.

> 예 · I like to play baseball.
> · I like to study English.

■ Would you like me to ~?와 같이 me가 들어가면 본인의 행동을 제안하는 표현이 됩니다.
(제가 ~해드릴까요?)

> 예 · Would you like me to hang your coat in the coatroom?

Review Test

1. Write the meaning of the following words.

   1) aboard _____

   2) immediately _____

   3) lavatory _____

   4) shortly _____

   5) instead _____

   6) inconvenience _____

   7) bassinet _____

   8) diaper _____

   9) appreciate _____

   10) overhead bin _____

   11) regulation _____

   12) on board _____

2. Complete the sentences with the correct words. Change the word form if necessary.

mind	during	see	care to	clear	return

   1) I'm sorry but we have to keep the aisle _____ .

   2) Would you _____ change seats so they can sit together?

   3) If you need anything _____ the flight, just let us know.

   4) I'll _____ if it can be arranged after take-off.

   5) Would you mind _____ your seat back to the upright position?

   6) Would you _____ keeping your bags under your seat, please?

3. Fill in the blank(s) with suitable word(s).

1) May I help you _____ your bag?

2) I'm _____ you're in the wrong seat.

3) Would you _____ for something to drink?

4) I'm sorry but I must _____ you _____ fasten your seat belt for take-off.

5) If you need further assistance, please _____ us know.

4. Translate the following into English.

1) 금방 가져다 드리겠습니다.

   _____.

2) 기다리시게 해서 죄송합니다.

   _____.

3) 이륙을 한 후에 화장실을 이용해 주시겠습니까?

   _____.

4) 불편을 끼쳐드려 대단히 죄송합니다.

   _____.

5) 이륙한 후에 확인해서 알려드리겠습니다.

   _____.

6) 가방을 옷장에 보관해드려도 괜찮으시겠습니까?

   _____.

Unit 03

En Route Service 비행 중의 서비스

1. Earphone and Towel Service(이어폰과 물수건 서비스)

승무원은 서비스 전 항공기 기종별로 제공되는 각 채널별 음악의 내용 및 영화에 관한 승객의 문의에 대비하여 해당 비행편의 음악 채널, 영상물의 종류 및 상영순서를 미리 확인한다. 담당 구역의 승객 수만큼 이어폰과 물수건을 미리 준비하고, 카트(cart)를 이용하여 서비스하며 승객이 적을 때는 트레이(tray)로 승객에게 이어폰 사용법을 설명하며 서비스 한다.

이어폰 서비스가 끝나면 물수건을 뜨겁게 데워 담당 통로별로 서비스 한다. 손바닥으로 바스켓의 아래 부분을 받치고 집게(tong)를 이용해서 물수건이 말아진 상태로 서비스 한다. 서비스 직전에 물수건의 온도, 습도, 냄새를 다시 한번 확인하고 서비스 후에는 바로 회수하여 정·위치에 보관 후 하기한다.

Words & Phrases

- tong : 집게, 부젓가락
- distribution : 배포, 분배
  ↔ pick-up : 수거, 회수
- We'll be serving breakfast soon. : 곧 아침식사가 제공됩니다.
- show : (영화, 방송 등을) 상영하다, 상영되다
- May I take your towel? : 물수건을 가져가도/치워도 될까요?
- en route : 비행중인, 도중에
- right after : ~바로 뒤에, 직후에

1) Earphone Service(이어폰 서비스)

Dialogue ❶

F : Flight attendant / **P** : Passenger

F : Excuse me. Here's your earphone set.

P : No, thank you. I don't want to buy one.

F : Oh, no, sir. It's free.

Dialogue ❷

F : Flight attendant / **P** : Passenger

F : Excuse me. Would you care for an earphone set?

P : Do you charge for it?

F : No, sir. It's free of charge.

P : O.K. I'll have one.

F : Here it is. Have a nice flight.

Notes

- It's free.
= It's free of charge.(무료입니다)
- charge : 돈을 받다. 청구하다

2) Towel Service(물수건 서비스)

Distribution

Dialogue ❶

F : Flight attendant / P : Passenger

F : Would you care for a hot towel?

Please be careful. It's very hot.

Towel pick-up

Dialogue ❷

F : Flight attendant / P : Passenger

F : Excuse me. May I take your towel, please?

P : Yes, thanks.

F : You're welcome.

Sleeping passenger who has no 'Do not disturb' sign

Dialogue ❸

F : Flight attendant / P : Passenger

F : Would you care for a hot towel?

We'll be serving breakfast soon.

Notes

· serve : (식사를) 제공하다

3) Movie Information Request(영화 정보 요청)

Dialogue ❶

F : Flight attendant / P : Passenger

F : Excuse me. Here's your earphone set.

P : Thanks. What movie are you showing today?

F : We're going to show 'Men In Black 3'. You can refer to the entertainment
      guide book in the seat pocket for the programs.

P : I see. Thanks.

F : My pleasure. Enjoy the movie.

4) Movie Time Information(영화 상영 시간 정보)

Dialogue ❶

F : Flight attendant / P : Passenger

P : Excuse me. When are you showing the movie today?

F : The movie will be shown in about one hour.

P : Thanks.

F : You're welcome.

Dialogue ❷
F : Flight attendant / P : Passenger

P : Excuse me. When are you showing the movie today?

F : The movie will be shown right after the meal.

P : Thanks.

F : You're welcome. Enjoy the movie.

Notes

· in : (시간의 경과를 나타냄) ~후에, ~만에, ~있으면
 → 현재(말하는 시점)부터 시작하여 앞으로 얼마 후를 의미
 ex The bus arrives in five minutes.(5분 후에, 5분 있으면)
    We arrives in Singapore in about 40 minutes.(약 40분 후)
 ※ 'after'는 보통 과거시제와 함께 쓰임
· right after : ~바로 후에

2. Meal and Beverage Services(식음료 서비스)

식전음료(Aperitif)는 식욕을 돋구는 개념으로 항공사에 따라 서비스 방법에 약간의 차이는 있지만 대체적으로 출발시간과 비행시간, 그리고 식사 시간대에 따라 트레이(tray) 또는 카트(cart)를 이용해 서비스 한다. 서비스 시에는 승객에게 제공되는 음료의 종류를 간략하게 설명한 후 주문을 받는다. 이 때 맥주, 와인류는 차갑게 냉장(chilling)된 상태로 서비스 하고, 탄산음료는 얼음을 넣어 차갑게 제공한다.

기내식(Meal Service)은 비행 중 승객에게 제공되는 음식으로 항공기 출발 전 항공사의 케이터링(catering)에 의해 고유의 음식을 이용하여 기내 주방(galley)에 보관하였다가 서비스 한다. 기내식 서비스가 끝나면 뜨거운 음료 서비스 준비를 확인하고, 물과 와인을 서비스 한다. 서비스 전에 와인의 품명 및 특성을 확인한 후 와인 서비스 요령에 따라 와인을 서비스 한다. 와인을 서비스 할 때는 승객이 선택한 와인을 간략히 소개하고 잔의 2/3까지 따르고, 따른 후에는 눈을 맞추고(eye contact) 미소를 짓는다.

와인과 물 서비스가 끝나면 뜨거운 음료(hot beverage)를 서비스 한다. 커피는 신선한 맛을 위해 서비스 직전에 우려내어 준비한다. 커피 포트 내외부의 청결상태를 확인 후 뜨거운 물로 데워서 준비한다.

승객의 식사가 90% 이상이 끝났을 때 밀 트레이의 회수를 시작하며, 회수 때에는 반드시 승객의 의사를 묻는다. 밀 서비스와 동일한 순서로 회수하고, 회수 시 깨끗하지 않은 승객의 테이블은 준비한 순서대로 닦는다. 회수 속도는 승객의 상황에 따라 다른 점에 유의하여 승객이 충분한 여유를 가지고 식사할 수 있도록 한다. 식사 제공 시에는 창가 좌석부터 중간석, 복도 좌석 순으로 서비스하고 트레이를 승객의 머리 위로 제공하지 않도록 한다.

Words & Phrases

- What would you like?
  = What would you care for?(무엇을 드시겠습니까?)
- Would you like cream or sugar? : 크림이나 설탕을 넣어드릴까요?
- How would you like your coffee/martini? : 커피/마티니는 어떻게 드시겠습니까?
- Have you finished (with) your drink/meal? : 음료/식사는 다 드셨습니까?
  → with는 생략 가능
- bulkhead : 칸막이
- arrange : (식사 등을) 준비하다. 정리하다
- entree : 주요리, 앙뜨레
- vegetarian meal : 채식
- get something to wipe it up : 닦을 것을 가져오다
- aperitif[a:pèrətí:f] : 식전주

1) Beverage Service(음료 서비스)

Basic situation

Dialogue ❶

F : Flight attendant / P : Passenger

F : Good morning, ma'am. Would you care for something to drink?

P : Yes, I'll have a beer. Do you have Heineken?

F : Certainly, ma'am. Here is your beer. Enjoy your drink.

Dialogue ❷

F : Flight attendant / P : Passenger

F : Would you like something to drink?
     We have orange juice, coke, coffee and tea. What would you like?

P : I'll have a cup of coffee.

F : Yes, sir. Would you like cream or sugar?

OR

How would you like your coffee?
Here you are.

Special request 1

Dialogue ❸

F : Flight attendant / P : Passenger

F : Good afternoon, sir. Would you care for something to drink?

P : What kind of juice do you have?

F : We have orange juice, apple juice and tomato juice, sir.

P : Apple juice, please.

F : Certainly, sir. Here is your apple juice. Enjoy your drink.

Special request 2

Dialogue ❹
F : Flight attendant / P : Passenger

F : Good evening, sir. Would you care for something to drink?
   We have juices, soft drinks, beers, coffee and tea.

P : Is that all you have?

F : No, sir. What would you care for, sir?

P : Can I have a martini?

F : Certainly. How would you like your martini?

P : I would like a Vodka Martini up.

F : Just a moment, sir. Here is your martini. Enjoy your drink.

Cocktail request

Dialogue ❺
F : Flight attendant / P : Passenger

F : Good evening, sir. Would you care for something to drink?
   We have liquors, juices, soft drinks and beers.

P : Do you have vodka?

F : Certainly, sir. How would you like your vodka, sir?

P : Vodka and tonic, please.

F : Certainly. Just a moment, please. Here is your vodka and tonic. Enjoy your drink.

Others

Dialogue ⑥

F : Flight attendant / P : Passenger

F : Good evening, ma'am. Would you like to have something to drink?
We have liquors, juices, soft drinks and beers.

P : Can I have a gin and tonic?

F : Certainly, ma'am. Just a moment, please.
Here is your gin and tonic. Enjoy your drink.

Unavailable beverage request

Dialogue ⑦

F : Flight attendant / P : Passenger

F : Excuse me. Would you like something to drink?

P : Do you have mango juice?

F : I'm sorry, but I'm afraid we don't have mango juice on board. We only
have orange, apple and pineapple juice.
What would you care for, ma'am?

P : Alright. Pineapple juice, please.

F : Certainly, ma'am. Here is your pineapple juice. Enjoy your drink.

Refill: Drink not on tray

Dialogue ⑧

F : Flight attendant / P : Passenger

P : Excuse me. Could I have another drink, please?

F : Certainly, sir. What would you care for, sir?

P : Another martini, please.

F : I'll get one for you soon.

(After a while)

Here is your martini. May I take your glass, sir?

Refill: Available on tray

Dialogue ❾
F : Flight attendant / P : Passenger

P : Excuse me. Can I have another beer, please?

F : Certainly. Here you are. May I take your glass, sir?

Cart service

Dialogue ❿
F : Flight attendant / P : Passenger

F : Good evening, ma'am.

  Would you care for something to drink before dinner, ma'am?

P : I'll have a scotch on the rock, please.

F : Certainly, ma'am. Here is your scotch on the rock. Enjoy your drink.

Strong and weak

Dialogue ⓫
F : Flight attendant / P : Passenger

P : Excuse me. My drink is too strong.

F : I'm sorry, sir. I'll add some more tonic.

Just a moment, please. Here's your drink.

How's it this time, sir?

P : Oh, that's better.

F : I'm sorry for the inconvenience. Enjoy your drink.

Wine and liquor service / Short flight

Dialogue ⑫

F : Flight attendant / P : Passenger

P : Do you offer any wine with lunch?

F : I'm sorry, but I'm afraid we don't offer wine on this flight.

Would you care for some scotch, instead?

Collection: Passenger finished with his / her glass

Dialogue ⑬

F : Flight attendant / P : Passenger

F : Excuse me. May I take your glass?

P : Sure.

F : Thank you, sir.

Collection: Passenger not finished

Dialogue ⑭

F : Flight attendant / P : Passenger

F : Excuse me. Have you finished with your drink?

P : No, I haven't finished yet.

F : I'm sorry, sir. Would you care for another one?

Bar closed prior to landing

Dialogue ⑮

F : Flight attendant / P : Passenger

P : Excuse me. Can I have another drink?

F : I'm sorry, but we've closed the bar in preparation for landing.

> **Notes**
>
> • **Would you care for + 명사** : ~를 드릴까요?/드시겠습니까?
>   = Would you like + 명사
>   cf Would you care to~
>   = Would you like to~(~하시겠습니까?)
> • Is that all you have?
>   = Is that all?
>   = That's it?(그게 전부인가요?)
> • How's it this time? : 이번에는 어떠세요?
> • in preparation for~ : ~준비를 위해

2) Meal Service(식사 서비스)

Short Flight Meal Service(단거리 식사 서비스)

Bulkhead / Front row passenger at meal time

Dialogue ①

F : Flight attendant / P : Passenger

F : Excuse me. We'll be serving lunch / dinner soon.
     Would you please open the tray table?
     Thank you. I hope you enjoy your meal.

Normal

Dialogue ❷

F : Flight attendant / P : Passenger

F : Excuse me. Would you mind opening your tray table, please?

Here is your meal. It's beef.

I hope you enjoy your meal.

During meal service

Dialogue ❸

F : Flight attendant / P : Passenger

P : Could I have some coffee, please?

F : Certainly, sir. Another attendant will serve coffee shortly.

Meal information request

Dialogue ❹

F : Flight attendant / P : Passenger

P : What's the meal today?

F : We have shrimp tempura today, ma'am.

P : I don't really like seafood of any kind.
Don't you have anything else?

F : I'm sorry, but I'm afraid we only offer shrimp on this flight.

P : Alright. I'll have the meal then.

F : I'm sorry. Here's your shrimp tempura. I hope you enjoy your meal.

P : Thank you.

F : You're welcome.

Delayed meal request

Dialogue ❺

F : Flight attendant / P : Passenger

P : I'm not really hungry right now. Could I have my meal later on during the
flight?

F : Certainly, ma'am. We could arrange your meal if you tell us within one
hour.
We are scheduled to arrive in Singapore in an hour and 40 minutes.

P : Thank you.

Dialogue ⑥

F : Flight attendant / P : Passenger

P : Excuse me. Could I have my meal later on during the flight?

F : I'm sorry, sir. We are going to land in 40 minutes. Would you care to have your meal now?

Coffee or tea service

Dialogue ⑦

F : Flight attendant / P : Passenger

F : Would you care for some coffee?

P : Yes, please.

F : May I have your cup, please? Thank you. Here's your coffee.

P : Can I have some cream and sugar?

F : Certainly, ma'am. Here you are.

Dialogue ⑧

F1 : Flight attendant 1 / F2 : Flight attendant 2 / P : Passenger

F1 : Would you care for some coffee?

P : Can I have some tea?

F1 : Certainly. Another attendant will serve tea shortly.

(After a while)

F2 : Would you care for some tea?

P : Yes, please.

F2 : May I have your cup, please? Thank you.
Would you care for some lemon?

P : No, thanks.

F2 : Here is your tea. Enjoy your drink.

Extra coffee and tea offer / Tray pick-up time: Short flight

Dialogue ❾
F : Flight attendant / P : Passenger

F : Would you care for some more coffee?

P : Yes, please.

F : May I have your cup, please?
Thank you. Here you are.

Dialogue ❿
F : Flight attendant / P : Passenger

F : Would you care for some more tea?

P : No, thanks.

F : May I take your meal tray?

P : Yes, please.

F : I hope you enjoyed your meal.

P : Yes, it was great.

F : I'm glad to hear that.

Dialogue ⑪

F : Flight attendant / P : Passenger

F : Would you care for some more coffee?

P : No, thanks.

F : Have you finished with your meal?

P : No, I'm not finished yet.

F : Oh, I am sorry. Please take your time and enjoy your meal.

● OPENING A BOTTLE OF WINE

Remove the top of the capsule by cutting round below the lip of the bottle.

This can be done either with a capsule remover or knife.

* Clean the neck of the bottle with a clean cloth.

* Draw the cork as gently and cleanly as possible using your selected corkscrew.

* Give the neck of the bottle a final clean inside and out.

Normal

Dialogue ❶

F : Flight attendant / **P1** : Passenger / **P2** : Passenger

F : Good evening. We have a choice of beef steak and Chinese style shrimp. Which one would you care for, ma'am?

P1: Um... I'd like the steak.

F : Certainly, ma'am.

Would you mind opening your tray table, please? Here's your steak.

(To P2)

How about you, sir?

P2: I'll have the shrimp.

F : Certainly, sir. Here is your shrimp.

Would you care for some wine?

P1: Yes, please.

F : Red or white wine?

P1: Red, please.

F : Here's your wine.

F : How about you, sir?

P2: Red wine, please.

F : Here's your wine.

Beef entree unavailable

Dialogue ②

F : Flight attendant / P : Passenger

F : Here is your meal.

P : Oh, excuse me. What kind of meal is this?

F : It's Chinese style shrimp, sir.

P : Um... I don't want Chinese style shrimp. Do you have any steak?

F : I'm sorry, but I'm afraid that we've run out of the steak.

P : I see.

F : I'm sorry, sir. I hope you enjoy your meal.

Special meal situations

Dialogue ③

F : Flight attendant / P : Passenger

P : Excuse me. When I made my reservation, I requested a Kosher meal.

F : I'm sorry, sir. May I have your name, please?

P : My name is Simon Baker.

F : Thank you. I'll check on your meal immediately.

(After a while)

Thank you for waiting. We have your kosher meal. May I unwrap your meal box and heat it up for you?

P : Yes, please.

F : We'll be heating up your meal and it'll be ready in about 20 minutes.

(20 minutes later)

Here's your meal. I'm sorry for the inconvenience.
Enjoy your meal, sir.

Special meal requested / not loaded

Dialogue ❹

F : Flight attendant / P : Passenger

P : Excuse me. I requested a vegetarian meal when I made my reservation.

F : I'm sorry, ma'am. May I have your name, please?

P : My name is Alice Lee.

F : Thank you. I'll check on your meal immediately.

(After a while)

I'm very sorry, but your meal wasn't loaded in Seoul. Our ground staff made a mistake.
May I offer another choice? Would you care for a vegetable salad, ma'am?

P : Well, all right.

F : Certainly, ma'am. I'll get one for you right away.

(After a while)

Here's your salad. I'm sorry for the inconvenience. I hope you enjoy your meal.

Something unpleasant in the food

Dialogue ❺

F : Flight attendant / P : Passenger

P : Excuse me. Look at this. How did this hair get in my meal?
You can't expect me to eat this.

F : I'm very sorry, ma'am. I'll get you another meal.

(After a while)

Thank you for waiting. Here's your meal.
Please accept our apologies. Can I get you anything else?

Additional food request in the economy class section

Dialogue ❻

F : Flight attendant / P : Passenger

P : Excuse me. This chicken was just delicious.
Do you have any more left over?

F : I'm glad you liked it. I'll go and check.

(After a while)

I'm sorry, but I'm afraid we don't have any chicken left.
Would you care for some more bread rolls?

Spill situation

Dialogue ❼

F : Flight attendant / P : Passenger

F : I'm terribly sorry, ma'am. I'll get something to wipe it up.

(After a while)

Would you like me to wipe it up for you?

P : No, that's all right. I can manage it.

F : Please accept my apology. We have a cleaning coupon. Would you please accept it, ma'am? You may take it to any Asiana Airlines office for reimbursement.
I'm terribly sorry, ma'am.

Lukewarm meal

Dialogue ❽

F : Flight attendant / P : Passenger

F : I don't think this meal is hot enough.

P : I'm sorry, sir. I'll heat it up for you.

(After a while)

Here's your meal. I'm sorry for the inconvenience. Would you care for something to drink, sir?

Passenger not hungry

Dialogue ❾

F : Flight attendant / P : Passenger

F : Which one would you care for, sir?

We have a choice of chicken and fish.

P : No, thank you. I'm not really hungry.

F : Then, would you care for some salad, instead?

P : No, that's alright.

F : Alright, sir.

Notes

- not ~ really
  = not ~ very(별로/그다지 ~ 않다)
- later on
  = later(나중에)
- be scheduled to ~ : ~할 예정이다
- in an hour and 40 minutes : 1시간 40분 후에/있으면
- be going to ~ : ~할 것이다
- May I have your cup? : 컵을 건네주시겠습니까?
  cf May I take your cup?(컵을 가져가도/치워도 되겠습니까?)
- take your time : (서두르지 말고) 천천히 하세요
- have a choice of ~ : ~중에 선택할 수 있다
- How about you, sir? : 손님은 어떠세요?(무엇을 드시겠습니까?)
- run out of ~ : 다 떨어지다. 바닥나다
- Kosher meal : 유대교식 식사
- heat up : 데우다
- be ready : 준비되다
  cf get ready for : ~를 준비하다
- load : (차, 비행기 등에 짐을) 싣다. 얹다
- ground staff : 지상 직원
- expect + 사람 + to ~ : …가 ~하기를 기대하다
- Please accept our apologies. : 부디 사죄를 받아주십시오.
- additional : 추가적인
- left over : 남은 것. 나머지
- I'm glad you liked it. : 마음에 드신다니 다행입니다.
- I can manage it.
  = I can handle it.(제가 할 수 있습니다.)
- reimbursement : 변상. 보상
- lukewarm : 미지근한

1. Write the meaning of the following words.

    1) lukewarm _____

    2) distribution _____

    3) reimbursement _____

    4) bulkhead _____

    5) preparation _____

    6) Kosher meal _____

    7) arrange _____

    8) entree _____

    9) load _____

    10) wipe _____

2. Complete the sentences with the correct words. Change the word form if necessary.

| run out of | care to | on board | in preparation for |
| arrange | take | | |

    1) I'm sorry, but we've closed the bar _____ landing.

    2) We could _____ your meal if you tell us within an hour.

    3) I'm sorry, but I'm afraid that we've _____ the steak.

    4) Please _____ your time and enjoy your meal.

    5) I'm afraid we don't have mango juice _____ .

    6) Would you _____ have your meal now?

3. Fill in the blank(s) with suitable word(s).

   1) We have orange juice, coke, coffee and tea. What _____ you
       _____ ?

   2) We are going to land _____ 40 minutes.

   3) Please _____ our apologies.

   4) **P** : Do you charge for it?

       F : No, sir. It's _____ of charge.

   5) We'll be _____ breakfast soon.

   6) _____ would you like your martini?

4. Translate the following into English.

   1) 마실 것 좀 가져다 드릴까요?

       _____.

   2) 잔을 치워도 될까요?

       _____.

   3) 식사는 다 드셨습니까?

       _____.

   4) 커피는 어떻게 타 드릴까요?

       _____.

   5) 1시간 40분 후에 싱가포르에 도착할 예정입니다.

       _____.

3. In-Flight Music and Movie(기내 음악과 영화)

기내 식사 서비스 후 승객들은 엔터테인먼트 서비스(음악과 영화)를 받게 된다. 항공사별로 비행시간에 따라 정해진 영화 및 단편물을 상영하게 되는데 최근에는 엔터테인먼트 시스템의 발달로 대형화면 이외에도 개인 모니터를 통해 여러편의 영화를 감상할 수도 있다. 영화 상영 전에 승무원은 승객의 영화관람 준비상태를 확인한 후 안내방송을 실시하고 담당구역(zone)별로 조명을 조절한다. 이 때 창문 가리개(window shade)를 내리고 이어폰이나 헤드폰을 다시 한번 서비스 한다. 사용채널이나 영화제목을 안내방송하고 전 객실내의 화면 상태를 점검한다. 또한 이어폰 사용 방법을 잘 모르는 승객을 도와주고 독서를 원하는 승객을 위해서는 독서등을 켤 수 있도록 서비스 하고 안내한다.

1) Music

Dialogue ❶

F : Flight attendant / **P** : Passenger

P : What kind of music do you have?

F : Well, we have pop, rock, jazz and classical music.
This pamphlet will show you today's in-flight music program.

2) Movie

Dialogue ❶

F : Flight attendant / **P** : Passenger

P : When are you showing the movie today?

F : The movie will be shown right after the meal, in about 2 hours and 10 minutes.

> **Notes**
> • in-flight : (형용사) 기내~
> • right after : ~ 직후에

4. Earphone Set Problems(이어폰 관련 문제)

Words & Phrases

- out of order
  = not working(고장난)
- I'm sorry to bother you. : 방해해서 죄송합니다.
- be willing to ~ : 기꺼이 ~하다
- I'll see what I can do. : 제가 알아보겠습니다.
- Are you going to ~? : ~하실 건지요?

1) Out of Order / Seat Available(시스템 고장 / 좌석 이동)

Dialogue ❶

F : Flight attendant / P : Passenger

P : Excuse me. I think my earphones aren't working.

F : Excuse me, sir. Let me check it. Can you hear it now?

P : No, still nothing at all.

F : Just a moment, please.

   (After a while)

   Would you like to move to this seat over here, sir?

   The sound system works fine here.

Notes

- **nothing at all** : 아무 것도 안들림
- **work fine** : 잘 작동되다

2) Out of Order / No Empty Seats Available
(시스템 고장 / 좌석이동 불가능)

Dialogue ❶

F : Flight attendant / **P1** : Passenger 1 / **P2** : Passenger 2

P1: Excuse me. This earphones are out of order.

F : Excuse me, sir. Can you hear it now?

P1: No, still nothing at all.

F : Just a moment, please. I'll see what I can do.

(After a while)

I'm sorry, but I'm afraid that all the seats are occupied.
Would you care for a newspaper or magazine?

P1: No, thanks. Is there any way of listening to music?

F : Wait a second, please. I'll see what I can do.

(To P2)

F : Excuse me. I'm sorry to bother you. Will you be listening to music, ma'am?

P1: No, I'll be reading most of the time. Why?

F : We have a passenger right over there who would like to listen to music, but the sound system in his seat is out of order.
Would you care to change seats with him?

P2: Sure. No problem.

F : Thank you very much. This way, please.

(To P1)

F : Excuse me. This lady is willing to change seats with you.

This way, please. Here's your seat.

(To P2)

F : Thank you very much. Is there anything I can get for you? Would you care
for a newspaper or a drink, ma'am?
I'm sorry for the inconvenience, ma'am.

P2 : That's all right.

F : Thank you again. I hope you enjoy the flight.

Dialogue ❷

F : Flight attendant / P : Passenger

P : Excuse me. I think my earphones are not working.

F : Excuse me, sir. Let me check it. Can you hear it now?

P : No, still not working.

F : Just a moment, please. I'll see what I can do.

(After a while)

I'm sorry, but I'm afraid that all the seats are occupied.

P : Oh, that's O.K. Don't worry.

F : I'm sorry, sir. Would you care for a newspaper or something to drink?

P : No, thanks.

F : If you need anything during the flight, please let me know.

Notes

· I'll see ∼ : ∼를 확인하겠습니다.
· most of the time : 대부분
· be willing to ∼ : 기꺼이 ∼하다

3) Bulkhead Passenger at Movie Time(스크린 앞쪽 승객)

Empty seat available

Dialogue ❶

F : Flight attendant / **P** : Passenger

F : Excuse me, sir. Are you going to watch the movie?

P : Yes.

F : I'm afraid you won't be able to see the screen very well from the seat. Would you like to change seats? We have some empty seats in the middle of the cabin.

P : Sounds good.

F : This way, please. Here's your seat. I hope you enjoy the movie.

No seat available: Passenger requests seat change

Dialogue ❷

F : Flight attendant / **P** : Passenger

P : Excuse me. I can't see the movie screen from this seat. Is there any empty seat in the middle of the cabin?

F : I'm sorry, but I am afraid all the seats are occupied.
I'm sorry for the inconvenience.

Notes

- Are you going to ~ ? : ~하실 건지요?
- won't be able to ~ : ~할 수 없을 것이다

5. In-Flight Sales(기내 면세품 판매)

　기내면세품 판매는 각 항공사의 중요 기내 서비스 중의 하나이다. 일반 매장 판매가는 물론 시내나 공항 면세점 보다 약 5~10% 싼 가격으로 우수한 상품을 구입할 수 있고, 해외 여행지에서 선물을 들고 다녀야 하는 불편함 없이 입국 항공기에서도 편안하게 구입할 수 있어서 여행객들이 선호한다. 일반적으로 식사 서비스가 끝나고 기내 면세품 판매에 관한 안내방송을 실시한 후 판매 담당 승무원들이 카트(cart)에 면세품을 준비하여 객실을 순회하며 구입을 원하는 승객에게 기내 면세품을 판매한다. 이 때 면세품의 종류 및 특성을 파악하여 기내 쇼핑지를 이용하여 정확한 가격을 안내하여야 한다. 면세품의 종류는 술, 담배, 화장품, 펜, 쵸코렛, 시계 등 다양하다. 승무원은 기내 면세품 판매를 위해 모든 종류의 외국통화 환전율을 숙지하고 있어야 한다.

　기내 면세품 판매 역시 서비스의 일부분이므로 휴식을 취하는 승객에게 방해가 되지 않도록 진행하는 것이 바람직하며, 기내 면세품 판매에 참여하지 않는 승무원은 담당 구역을 정기적으로 순회(walk around)하여 객실내의 안전 유지 및 승객의 욕구충족을 통해 항공여행의 쾌적성을 도모하도록 한다.

Words & Phrases

- duty-free items : 면세품
- liquors : 주류
- How would you like to pay? : 결제는 어떻게 하시겠습니까?
  = How will you be paying?
- traveler's check : 여행자 수표
- order : 주문, 주문한 것
- May I take your order for ~ ? : ~를 주문하시겠습니까?
- I'll get your order. : 주문하신 것을 가져오겠습니다.
- Here's your order. : 주문하신 것 여기 있습니다.
- I'm afraid it has sold out. : 죄송하지만 품절되었습니다.
- not in stock : 재고가 없는
- be allowed to : ~하는 것이 허용되다
- get a refund : 환불을 받다
- as soon as I can : 최대한 빨리

1) General(면세품 판매 상황)

Dialogue ❶

F : Flight attendant / P : Passenger

F : Excuse me, sir.

Would you like to purchase any duty-free items?

We have cosmetics, perfumes, liquors and some nice gift items.

What would you care for?

P : What kind of gift items do you have?

F : We have all kinds of gift items.

This shopping guide has all the information about our duty-free sales.

P : Do you know how much whiskey I can take into Hong Kong?

F : You're allowed one liter of liquor or wine duty-free.

P : Okay. Bring me two bottles of whiskey.

F : Certainly, sir.

What kind of whiskey would you care for?

We have Jonnie Walker Blue, Ballantine's 17 Years Old and Royal Salute 21 Years Old.

P : Two bottles of Ballantine's 17 Years Old, Please.

F : Two bottles of Ballantine's 17 Years Old, sir.

How would you like to pay, in cash or by credit card?

P : How about traveler's checks?

F : Certainly, sir.

Just countersign the check and write your name, passport number and nationality in the back.

One moment, please. I'll get your order.

(After a while)

I'm sorry to have kept you waiting, sir.

Here's your order.

Please double check your order. That will be $500.00 US dollars.

P : Here's 500 dollars in traveler's checks.

F : Thank you, sir.

Duty free allowance

Dialogue ❷
F : Flight attendant / P : Passenger

P : Excuse me. Do you know how much perfume I can take into Hong Kong?

F : This pamphlet will show you the duty free allowance for Hong Kong, ma'am.

You may take up to 70 milliliters of perfume.

P : Oh, I see. Thanks.

F : You're welcome.

Notes

- gift items : 선물 제품
- be allowed ~ : ~가 허용되다
- countersign : 연서하다
- nationality : 국적
- in the back : 뒷면에
- duty free allowance : 면세품 허용량
- refund : 환불
  → get a refund(환불을 받다)
- up to : ~까지

2) Sales Items Request(면세품 주문)

Dialogue ❶

F : Flight attendant / P : Passenger

F : Excuse me, would you like to buy any duty free items, ma'am?

P : Yes, what kind of cosmetics do you sell?

F : We have Lancome, Chanel, Dior, etc.

You may refer to this shopping guide book. It shows what kind of cosmetics we sell.

Dialogue ❷

F : Flight attendant / P : Passenger

F : What would you like, sir?

P : Um..... What kind of liquor do you sell?

F : We have Johnnie Walker Black, Ballantine 17, Chivas Regal and Camus.

Dialogue ❸

F : Flight attendant / P : Passenger

F : May I help you?

P : Yes, what kind of perfume do you sell?

F : We have Nina Ricci, Christian Dior and Chanel.

P : Fine. I'll take Christian Dior.

F : Yes, ma'am. Would you like perfume for a female or a male?

P : I'd like to get Homme perfume.

F : How would you like to pay, ma'am?

P : Can I pay by credit card?

F : Certainly, ma'am.

In-Flight sales / Order base

Dialogue ④
F : Flight attendant / P : Passenger

F : May I take your order for any duty-free items, sir?

P : Yes, what do you have?

F : We have liquors, various gift items, cosmetics, cigarettes and perfumes for sale.

This shopping guide has all the information about our in-flight sales.

Notes

• etc [etsetərə] : ~ 등등
  = and so on
• take one's order : 주문을 받다

3) In-Flight Sales(면세품 판매)

Exact change received

Dialogue ❶

F : Flight attendant / **P** : Passenger

F : Excuse me, would you like to buy any duty-free items, ma'am?

P : Could I have a bottle of Johnnie Walker Black?

F : Certainly, ma'am. Here you are, ma'am. That will be $60.00, please.

P : Here's one hundred dollars.

F : Thank you. Here's your change, $40.00.

Passenger gives large bill / Change unavailable

Dialogue ❷

F : Flight attendant / **P** : Passenger

P : I'm sorry, but all I have is a 100 dollar bill. Do you have change?

F : I'm sorry, but I'm afraid I don't have change right now.
I will bring your change as soon as I can. Would that be alright, sir?

F : No problem.

(After a while)

P : I'm sorry to have kept you waiting, sir. Here's your change, $30.00. Is that correct, sir?

F : Yes, it's correct. Thanks.

P : My pleasure.

Passenger gives tip

Dialogue ③
F : Flight attendant / P : Passenger

P : You may keep the change.

F : I'm sorry, ma'am, but I'm afraid we are not allowed to accept any tip.

Dialogue ④
F : Flight attendant / P : Passenger

P : You may keep the change.

F : I'm sorry, but I can't. We are not allowed to accept any tip.

Item is sold out or not in stock on the flight

Dialogue ⑤
F : Flight attendant / P : Passenger

P : Excuse me. I'd like to buy a bottle of Chivas Regal, please.

F : I'm sorry, ma'am, but I'm afraid it has sold out.
　　Would you care for a bottle of Camus, instead?

P : Yes, all right.

F : Certainly, ma'am. That will be $47.00. Thank you.

Dialogue ⑥
F : Flight attendant / P : Passenger

P : Excuse me. I'd like to buy a bottle of Chivas Regal, please.

F : I'm sorry, sir, but I'm afraid it has sold out.
Would you like a bottle of Camus, instead?

P : No, thanks.

F : I'm sorry for the inconvenience, sir.

Passenger requests sales item before cart reaches their aisle

Dialogue ❼
F : Flight attendant / P : Passenger

P : I'd like to buy a bottle of Chanel No. 5, please.

F : I'll serve you as soon as I can, ma'am. Would you mind waiting until we
bring the cart to your seat, please? Thank you for your understanding.

Traveler's checks / Unacceptable currency

Dialogue ❽
F : Flight attendant / P : Passenger

P : Excuse me. Do you accept traveler's checks?

F : Yes, sir.

P : Here you are.

F : Thank you, sir. Please countersign here and write your name, passport
number and nationality on the back, sir.
Here is your change, 70 dollars, sir.

Dialogue ❾
F : Flight attendant / P : Passenger

P : Excuse me. Do you accept Chinese Renminbi?

F : I'm sorry, but I'm afraid we do not accept Renminbi, ma'am.

  We only accept U.S. dollars, European Euros, Korean won and Japanese yen.

Passenger asks for refund

Dialogue ⑩

F : Flight attendant / P : Passenger

P : Excuse me. Would I be able to get a refund on this perfume?

F : May I ask where you bought it, ma'am?

P : I bought it at the airport duty-free shop.

F : I'm sorry, but I'm afraid we can only give refunds on items purchased during the flight, ma'am.

Dialogue ⑪

F : Flight attendant / P : Passenger

P : Excuse me. Would I be able to get a refund on this perfume?

F : May I ask where you bought it, ma'am?

P : I bought it here, about 10 minutes ago.

F : Certainly, ma'am. Just a moment, please.

(After a while)

May I have the perfume?

Here's your refund, ma'am.

Passenger waiting for change

Dialogue ⑫

F : Flight attendant / **P** : Passenger

P : Excuse me. Where's my change?

F : I'm sorry to have kept you waiting, ma'am.
Here's your change, $20.00. Is that correct?

Dialogue ⑬

F : Flight attendant / **P** : Passenger

P : Excuse me. Where's my change?

F : I'm sorry. I still don't have change yet.
I'll bring your change as soon as possible, sir.

Notes

- change : 거스름돈, 잔돈
- Keep the change. : 잔돈은 가지세요.
- are not allowed to ~ : ~하는 것이 허용되지 않는다
- currency : 통화, 화폐

Review Test

1. Write the meaning of the following words.

   1) currency _____

   2) refund _____

   3) liquor _____

   4) in-flight _____

   5) purchase _____

   6) bother _____

   7) out of order _____

   8) traveler's check _____

   9) nationality _____

   10) change _____

2. Complete the sentences with the correct words. Change the word form if necessary.

in-flight	right after	willing	allow	take
wait	get			

   1) You're _____ one liter of liquor or wine duty-free.

   2) The movie will be shown _____ the meal.

   3) Would I be able to _____ a refund on this perfume?

   4) May I _____ your order for any duty-free items, sir?

   5) This pamphlet will show you today's _____ music program..

   6) Would you mind _____ until we bring the cart to your seat, please?

   7) This lady is _____ to change seats with you.

3. Fill in the blank(s) with suitable word(s).

1) I'm sorry, but I'm _____ we do not accept Lira, ma'am.

2) P : Excuse me. I think my earphones are not _____ .

   F : Let me check. Can you hear it now?

3) Just a moment, please. I'll _____ what I can do.

4) Just _____ the check and write your name, passport number and nationality in the back.

5) The movie will be shown right after the meal, _____ _____ 2 hours and 10 minutes.

6) I'm sorry to _____ _____ you waiting.

4. Translate the following into English.

1) 주문하신 것을 가져오겠습니다.

   _____.

2) 결제는 어떻게 하시겠습니까?

   _____.

3) 죄송합니다만 저희는 팁을 받을 수 없습니다.

   _____.

4) 이쪽에 있는 자리로 옮겨 앉으시겠습니까?

   _____.

5) 방해해서 죄송합니다.

   _____.

● 참고자료

1. 면세품 주문서

기내면세품 주문서 & 영수증　Duty Free Order Form & Receipt

- 이 주문서는 영수증으로 대처가능합니다. / 카드사용시 1카드당 사용가능한 카드한도 범위가 제한적이므로 기내면세책자를 참조해 주시기 바랍니다.
- 해외로부터 입국하는 내외국인상시면세권자 포함의 경우 1인당 미화 400불 초과 시는 세관신고 후 세금을 납부하셔야 합니다.
- 체크카드(CHECK CARD)및 직불카드(DEBIT CARD)는 개내접수가 불가하므로, 양해하여 주시기 바랍니다.
- 기내에서 예약주문을 하신 손님께서는 당승 후 승무원에게 예약주문 사본을 제시하여 주시기 바랍니다.
- 인천 -- 엔타이, 인천 -- 웨이하이, 인천 -- 다롄, 부산 -- 후쿠오카, 제주 -- 후쿠오카 구간은 예약주문으로만 기내면세품 구입이 가능합니다.

December 2008　12

사업자 등록번호 : 104-81-17480
상호명 : 아시아나항공(주)
대표자 : 강 주 안
주　소 : 서울시 강서구 오쇠동 47

◈ 기내주문(IN-FLIGHT ORDER)을 원하시는 분은 아래사항을 기입바랍니다.		접수 승무원	
기내주문 (IN-FLIGHT ORDER)	좌석번호(SEAT NO.)　성명(NAME)	전달 승무원	

◈ 현금지불시 : 원화/KRW　달러/USD　엔화/JPY　유로화/EUR　◈ 신용카드지불시 : 원화/KRW　달러/USD (　)　일시불　할부 (　개월)

다른 항공편으로 갈아타십니까?　Do you have any connecting flight?　□ 예(YES)　□ 아니오(NO)

◈ 예약주문(PRE-FLIGHT ORDER)을 원하시는 분은 아래사항을 기입바랍니다.

예약주문 (PRE-FLIGHT ORDER)	원지출발일(DATE)　2008/　월/(mm)　일/(dd)	성명(NAME)
	여객기출수편의광(FLT NO.)　접수승무원	전화번호(TEL)

- 판매가격은 상품을 전달받으시는 당승일을 기준으로 하며, 2009년 1월의 판매가격은 2008년 12월 가격과 상이할 수 있습니다.

일본 · 중국 · 러시아 노선 판매용 (sale on Japan, China, Russia Routes)　**No.**　일본 · 중국 · 러시아 · 동남아 일부 · 사이판 노선 소형 기종(B737/A321/A320) 운항시 판매용 (sale in small aircraft(B737/A321/A320) On Japan, China, Russia, some routes to Southeast Asia & Saipan)

	No.	ITEM	QTY 수량	USD	KRW	JPY	EUR		No.	ITEM	QTY 수량	USD	KRW	JPY	EUR
예약주문상품	900	Highland Park 30 Years Old		288	337,000	28,200	228	주류	21	Macallan Whisky Maker's Selection		81	95,900	7,900	64
	901	Longmorn 16		93	109,000	9,103	73		22	The Glenlivet Archive 21 Year Old		131	153,500	12,800	103
	902	Jackson-Triggs Cabernet Franc Ice Wine		115	134,500	11,300	91		23	Dalmore 1980		350	409,500	34,300	276
	903	Emporio Armani Men's Watch		236	276,000	23,103	186		24	Chivas Regal 25 Years Old		236	276,000	23,100	186
	904	Emporio Armani Ladies' Watch		236	276,000	23,100	186		100	Lancome Compact Mat Finish		29	34,000	2,800	23
	905	Swarovski Maldives Watch		385	450,500	37,700	304		101	Dior Dorissime Makeup Palette		66	77,000	6,500	52
	907	S.T.Dupont D-Link Ballpoint Pen		220	257,500	21,600	174		102	S/Ferragamo After Shave Set		42	49,000	4,100	33
	908	Waterman Carene Set		350	409,500	34,300	276		103	E/L Night Repair Eye		44	51,500	4,300	35
	909	Waterman Expert Set		185	216,500	18,100	146		104	E/L Complete Finish Compact		23	27,000	2,300	18
	910	Yamaha NX-U10 USB Powering Stereo Speaker		140	164,000	13,700	111		105	Sulwhasoo First Care Serum		53	62,000	5,200	42
	911	Ameth Necklace-Dream Of Flower		170	199,000	16,700	134		106	E/A Gold Capsules		34	40,000	3,300	27
	912	Aigner Diamond Ball Pendant		229	268,000	22,400	181		107	Burberry After Shave Skin		35	41,000	3,400	28
	913	Swarovski Short Diva Necklace		210	245,500	20,600	166		108	Lancome Absolue Seduction		48	56,000	4,700	38
	914	Tasaki Pearl Necklace (Milky Way)		395	462,000	38,700	312		109	Dior Lipstick La Collection		63	73,500	6,200	50
	915	Tasaki Pearl Pendant (Elegant)		779	911,500	76,300	615		110	L'Occitane Happiest Hands Kit		49	57,500	4,800	39
	916	Apron Beige(XL)		25	29,000	2,400	20		111	E/A Gold Eye Capsules		27	31,500	2,600	21
	918	Etro Arnica Line		333	389,500	32,600	263		112	Lancome Oil Virtuose Mascara		45	52,500	4,400	36
	919	Etro Arnica Boston Bag		491	574,500	48,100	388		113	Biotherm Homme Aquatic Lotion		35	41,000	3,400	28
	920	S.T.Dupont Men's Belt		175	204,500	17,103	138	화장품	114	Kanebo Dew Repair Mask		46	54,000	4,500	36
	921	MCM Aida Tote Bag		365	427,000	35,800	288		115	E/L Crystal Lip Jewels Trio		50	58,500	4,900	39
	922	MCM Visetos Marble Boston Small		312	365,000	30,600	246		116	Sulwhasoo Lifting Cream		53	62,000	5,200	42
	923	Dunhill Ideight C Small North South Bag		380	444,500	37,200	300		117	Givenchy Prismissime Compact		35	41,000	3,400	28
	924	Dunhill Sentryman Boc Ballford		314	367,500	30,800	248		119	Chanel Travel Makeup Palette		59	69,000	5,800	47
	925	Aigner Gents Rectangle Watch		249	291,500	24,400	197		120	Lancome UV Expert NEUROSHIELD		45	52,500	4,400	36
	926	Apron Red(XL)		24	28,000	2,400	19		121	Versace Compact		39	45,500	3,800	31
주류	1	Ballantine's 17 Years Old		58	68,000	5,700	46		122	Lancome Trio Color Fever Dewy Shine		64	75,000	6,300	51
	2	Ballantine's 21 Years Old		93	109,000	9,100	73		123	Polo Blue After Shave		41	48,000	4,000	32
	3	Royal Salute 21 Years Old		93	109,000	9,100	73		124	E/L Advanced Complex		73	85,500	7,200	58
	4	Ballantine's 30 Years Old		284	332,500	27,800	224		125	L'Occitane Rose Face Mist Duo		28	33,000	2,700	22
	5	Chivas Regal 18 Years Old		56	65,500	5,500	44		126	Guerlain Kiss Kiss Gloss Trio		59	69,000	5,800	47
	6	Johnnie Walker Blue		193	226,000	18,900	152	화장품	128	E/L Idealist Skin Refinisher		70	82,000	6,900	55
	7	Jackson-Triggs Vidal Icewine		59	69,000	5,800	47		129	Diorsnow Sublissime UV Base		43	50,500	4,200	34
	8	Remy Martin X.O Excellence		103	120,500	10,100	81		130	Anna Sui Mini Rouge (2pcs)		24	28,000	2,400	19
	9	Camus X.O Elegance		96	112,500	9,400	76		131	Clarins Pore Minimizing Serum		36	42,000	3,500	28
	10	Johnnie Walker Gold Label		59	69,000	5,800	47		132	Shiseido Eye Contour Cream		55	64,500	5,400	43
	11	Platinum Seal		48	56,000	4,700	38		133	Lancome Morpholift Eye Cream		63	73,500	6,200	50
	12	Dewar's 12 Years Old 1L		26	30,500	2,500	21		134	Dior Gaucho Lip Palette		49	57,500	4,800	39
	13	Glenfiddich 18 Years Old		56	65,500	5,500	44		135	Lancome Morpholift R.A.R.E Cream		100	117,000	9,800	79
	14	Johnnie Walker King George V		399	467,000	39,100	315		136	E/A Gift To Go Beauty Essentials		31	36,500	3,000	24
	15	Royal Salute 38 Years Old		399	467,000	39,100	315		137	O'Hui Intensive Sun Block Cake SPF 50+		31	36,500	3,000	24
	16	Royal Salute Hundred Cask		192	224,500	18,800	152		139	Zein Sanggi Sleeping Pack		31	36,500	3,000	24
	17	Landy X.O. No.1		90	105,500	8,800	71		140	Aramis After Shave		27	31,500	2,600	21
	18	Glenfiddich 21 Years Old		115	134,500	11,300	91		141	Gowoonseesang UV Suncream		25	29,000	2,400	20
	19	Blandy's Malmsey Madeira Wine		58	68,000	5,700	46		142	E/L Hydra Complete		38	44,500	3,700	30
	20	Remy Martin X.O Premier CRU		115	134,500	11,300	91		143	Guerlain Meteorite Mythic Trio		67	78,500	6,600	53

- 면세품 구입 및 A/S 관련 문의 : (080)669-3434(국내전화), (02)2669-3434
- 공동운항구간(OZ6401~6999, OZ9001~9999)은 예약주문 불가함.

구매액

2. 기내선물 서비스

● Giveaway Service (기내 선물 서비스)

F : It is a complimentary giveaway (gift) for children, courtesy of Asiana Airlines.
We have diary, pencil case and beach ball. Which one would you like?

F : Excuse me, Miss Johnson?
There are promotional gifts, courtesy of Asiana Airlines. We have a choice of ties,
memo pads, key holders and gentlemen's kit. Which one would you like?

P : Oh, really? Can I see that scarf?

F : Sure, here you are.

P : It's so pretty. I'll take this one. Thank you.

F : You're welcome. Miss Johnson. I am glad you like it.

6. Customs, Immigration and Quarantine
(세관, 입국 및 검역 안내서)

각 구역의 담당 승무원은 목적지 공항 도착 전 도착지 입국에 필요한 서류의 작성여부를 담당구역별로 재확인하고 승객의 미비한 서류작성을 돕는다.

목적지 공항의 세관 신고서, 입국 카드, 검역 안내서(Customs, Immigration and Quarantine) 절차에 대해서는 비행 전 정확한 내용을 숙지하여 고객안내에 차질이 없도록 한다. 국제선 단거리인 경우에는 안전에 저해되지 않는 경우 지상(ground)에서 서비스하고 장거리인 경우에는 기내 면세품 판매 후 담당구역별로 서비스 한다. 입국 서류 배포 시 승객의 경유(transit)여부나 최종 목적지를 확인하여 적합한 목적지 입국 서류를 배부한다. 특히 일정액 이상을 소지하고 입국하거나 고가의 물품을 구매한 승객은 반드시 세관신고서에 신고해야 한다. 참고로 북미(North America)를 제외한 다른 나라의 경우 통과 승객(transit passenger)은 CIQ절차를 거칠 필요가 없다.

Words & Phrases

- immigration : 입국(심사), 출입국 관리
- quarantine : 검역
- disembark : 하선하다
  - ↔ embark(승선하다)
- disembarkation card : 입국신고서
- Would you like me to help you with the card? : 신고서 작성하는 것을 도와드릴까요?
- customs declaration : 세관 신고
- take the city tour : 시내관광을 하다
- transit : 통과, 환승
  - transit area : 환승구역
  - transit without visa : 무사증통과

1) Disembarkation Card / Tourist(입국신고서 / 관광객)

Dialogue ❶

F : Flight attendant / **P** : Passenger

P : Excuse me. I'll be staying in Korea for one month.
Do I need to fill out this card?

F : Yes, ma'am. Foreigners entering Korea must fill out the disembarkation card. Here you are.
Would you like me to help you with it?

P : No, thanks.

F : Alright, ma'am.

- **need to** : ∼할 필요가 있다. ∼해야 한다(=have to)
  ↔ do not need to
- **fill out** : 작성하다. 기재하다

2) Embarkation & Disembarkation Card / Transit Passengers
(출국, 입국 신고서 / 통과 승객)

Dialogue ❶

F : Flight attendant / **P** : Passenger

P : Excuse me. I'll be at Incheon only for a few hours and then I'll be flying on to Hong Kong. Do I need this card?

F : No, sir. You don't need to fill out the card.

Dialogue ❷

F : Flight attendant / P : Passenger

P : I'm going to take the city tour of Seoul, and continue my flight this evening. Do I need this card?

F : Yes, ma'am. Please fill out the card and write "Transit" here.

Notes

- and then : 그런 다음, 그리고 나서.
- transit : 통과, 환승

3) Transit without Visa(무사증 통과)

Dialogue ❶

F : Flight attendant / P : Passenger

P : Excuse me. I'll be in Korea overnight, and I was told I didn't need a visa. Do I need to fill out this form?

F : Will you be leaving the transit area at the airport?

P : Yes.

F : Alright, sir. You must fill out the card. But please write "TWOV" in the 'Purpose of Travel' section.

＊ TWOV는 Transit Without Visa의 줄임말입니다.

Notes

- overnight : (부사) 하룻밤동안, 밤사이에
- be told (that) ~ : ~라고 듣다
- 'Purpose of Travel' section : '여행목적'란

4) Customs Declaration Card / Resident and Tourist
(세관신고서 / 거주자와 관광객)

Dialogue ❶

F : Flight attendant / P : Passenger

P : Excuse me. Will I need this card for Korea?

F : All passengers must fill out both sides of the card. Would you like me to help you with the card, sir?

P : No, thanks.

F : Alright, sir. Did you have a nice trip?

5) Customs Declaration Card / Passenger Given the Wrong Version Card(세관신고서 / 승객에게 잘못된 언어의 신고서 제공)

Dialogue ❶

F : Flight attendant / P : Passenger

P : Excuse me. What kind of card is this?

F : Oh, I'm sorry, ma'am. I'll get you one that's written in English. Just a moment, please.

(After a while)

Here you are, ma'am.

Would you like any help?

● 참고자료

1. 미국 세관신고서(영문)

U.S. Customs and Border Protection

Customs Declaration

19 CFR 122.27, 148.12, 148.13, 148.110,148.111, 1498; 31 CFR 5316

FORM APPROVED
OMB NO. 1515-0041

Each arriving traveler or responsible family member must provide the following information (only ONE written declaration per family is required):

1. **Family Name**
   First (Given)   Middle
2. **Birth date**   Day   Month   Year
3. Number of **Family members** traveling with you
4. (a) U.S. Street **Address** (hotel name/destination)

   (b) City   (c) State   California
5. **Passport issued by** (country)
6. **Passport number**
7. Country of **Residence**
8. **Countries visited** on this
   trip prior to U.S. arrival
9. **Airline/Flight No. or Vessel Name**
10. The primary purpose of this trip is **business**:   Yes   No
11. I am (We are) bringing
    (a) fruits, plants, food, insects: Yes   No
    (b) meats, animals, animal/wildlife products: Yes   No
    (c) disease agents, cell cultures, snails: Yes   No
    (d) soil or have been on a farm/ranch/pasture: Yes   No
12. I have (We have) been in close proximity of
    (such as touching or handling) livestock: Yes   No
13. I am (We are) carrying **currency or monetary**
    instruments over $10,000 U.S. or foreign equivalent: Yes   No
    (see definition of monetary instruments on reverse)
14. I have (We have) **commercial merchandise**:   Yes   No
    (articles for sale, samples used for soliciting orders,
    or goods that are not considered personal effects)
15. **Residents** — the **total value of all goods**, including commercial
    merchandise I/we have purchased or acquired abroad, (including gifts
    for someone else, but not items mailed to the U.S.) and am/are bringing
    to the U.S. is: $

    Visitors — the **total value of all articles** that will remain in the U.S.,
    including commercial merchandise is: $

Read the instructions on the back of this form. Space is provided to list all the items you must declare.

I HAVE READ THE IMPORTANT INFORMATION ON THE REVERSE SIDE OF THIS FORM AND HAVE MADE A TRUTHFUL DECLARATION.

X _____

(Signature)   Date (day/month/year)

For Official Use Only

CBP Form 6059B (10/07)

U.S. Customs and Border Protection Welcomes You to the United States

U.S. Customs and Border Protection is responsible for protecting the United States against the illegal importation of prohibited items. CBP officers have the authority to question you and to examine you and your personal property. If you are one of the travelers selected for an examination, you will be treated in a courteous, professional, and dignified manner. CBP Supervisors and Passenger Service Representatives are available to answer your questions. Comment cards are available to compliment or provide feedback.

Important Information

U.S. Residents — Declare all articles that you have acquired abroad and are bringing into the United States.

Visitors (Non-Residents) — Declare the value of all articles that will remain in the United States.

Declare all articles on this declaration form and show the value in U.S. dollars. For gifts, please indicate the retail value.

Duty — CBP officers will determine duty. U.S. residents are normally entitled to a duty-free exemption of $800 on items accompanying them. Visitors (non-residents) are normally entitled to an exemption of $100. Duty will be assessed at the current rate on the first $1,000 above the exemption.

Agricultural and Wildlife Products — To prevent the entry of dangerous agricultural pests and prohibited wildlife, the following are restricted: Fruits, vegetables, plants, plant products, soil, meat, meat products, birds, snails, and other live animals or animal products. Failure to declare such items to a Customs and Border Protection Officer/Customs and Border Protection Agriculture Specialist/Fish and Wildlife Inspector can result in penalties and the items may be subject to seizure.

Controlled substances, obscene articles, and toxic substances are generally prohibited entry.

Thank You, and Welcome to the United States.

The transportation of currency or **monetary instruments**, regardless of the amount, is legal. However, if you bring in to or take out of the United States more than $10,000 (U.S. or foreign equivalent, or a combination of both), you are required by law to file a report on FinCEN 105 (formerly Customs Form 4790) with U.S. Customs and Border Protection. Monetary instruments include coin, currency, travelers checks and bearer instruments such as personal or cashiers checks and stocks and bonds. If you have someone else carry the currency or monetary instrument for you, you must also file a report on FinCEN 105. Failure to file the required report or failure to report the *total* amount that you are carrying may lead to the seizure of *all* the currency or monetary instruments, and may subject you to civil penalties and/or criminal prosecution. SIGN ON THE OPPOSITE SIDE OF THIS FORM AFTER YOU HAVE READ THE IMPORTANT INFORMATION ABOVE AND MADE A TRUTHFUL DECLARATION.

Description of Articles (List may continue on another CBP Form 6059B)	Value	CBP Use Only
Total		

PAPERWORK REDUCTION ACT NOTICE: The Paperwork Reduction Act says we must tell you why we are collecting this information, how we will use it, and whether you have to give it to us. The information collected on this form is needed to carry out the Customs, Agriculture, and currency laws of the United States. CBP requires the information on this form to insure that travelers are complying with these laws and to allow us to figure and collect the right amount of duty and tax. Your response is mandatory. An agency may not conduct or sponsor, and a person is not required to respond to a collection of information, unless it displays a valid OMB control number. The estimated average burden associated with this collection of information is 4 minutes per respondent or record keeper depending on individual circumstances. Comments concerning the accuracy of this burden estimate and suggestions for reducing this burden should be directed to U.S. Customs and Border Protection, Reports Clearance Officer, Information Services Branch, Washington, DC 20229, and to the Office of Management and Budget, Paperwork Reduction Project (1651-0009), Washington, DC 20503. THIS FORM MAY NOT BE REPRODUCED WITHOUT APPROVAL FROM THE CBP FORMS MANAGER.

CBP Form 6059B (10/07)

미국 세관신고서(국문)

U.S. Customs and Border Protection

세관 신고서
19 CFR 122.27, 148.12, 148.13, 148.110, 148.111, 1498, 31 CFR 5316

허가 경식
OMB NO. 1651-0009

도착하시는 여행객 또는 가족의 책임자 되시는 분은 반드시 다음 정보를 제공해 주셔야 합니다. (신고서는 한 가족에 한 부만 기입하시면 됩니다.)

1. 성
   명   중간 이름

2. 생년월일   일   월   년

3. 본인과 동행하는 **가족 인원 수**

4. (a) 미국내 **주소:** 스트리트 (호텔 이름/목적지)

   (b) 시   (c) 주

5. 여권 발행 국가

6. 여권 번호

7. 거주 국가

8. 이번 여행 중 미국에 도착
   하기 전 **방문했던 국가**

9. 항공회사/탑승권 번호 또는 **선박 이름**

10. 이번 여행의 주요 목적은 **비즈니스** 입니다.   예   아니오

11. 나 (우리)는 다음 물품을 가지고 입국합니다
    (a) 과일, 채소, 식물, 종자, 식품, 곤충: 예   아니오
    (b) 육류, 동물, 동물/야생동물 제품: 예   아니오
    (c) 병원체, 세포배양물, 달팽이: 예   아니오
    (d) 흙을 소지하거나 농장/목장/목축장을 방문한 적이 있습니다   예   아니오

12. 나 (우리)는 **가축**과 가까이 한 적 (만지거나 다룬 적)이
    있습니다.   예   아니오

13. 나 (우리)는 미화 10,000 달러 이상, 또는 외화로
    그와 동등한 가치의 **통화나 화폐**를 휴대하고 있습니다.   예   아니오
    (뒷면의 화폐에 대한 정의를 참조하십시오.)

14. 나 (우리)는 다음의 **상업용 상품**을 휴대하고 있습니다.   예   아니오
    (판매용 물품, 주문 접수용 견본품, 또는 개인 소지품으로
    간주할 수 있는 물품)

15. **거주자** — 내/우리가 해외에서 구입 또는 취득하고 (타인을 위한 선물은
    포함되나 우편으로 미국에 보낸 것은 포함되지 않음) 지금 미국으로 가지고
    들어오는 **시판용 상품을** 포함한 모든 물품의 **총 가치:** $

    방문객 — 시판용 상품을 포함하여 미국에 남겨 두게될 **모든 물품의 총 가치:**
                                                              $

이 양식 뒷면의 설명문을 잘 읽으십시오. 반드시 신고해야 할 품목을 기입하실 수 있는 공간도 있습니다.

나는 이 양식의 뒷면에 있는 중요한 정보를 읽었으며 사실대로 신고하겠습니다.

X _____
(서명)   날짜 (일/월/년)

공무 전용란

CBP Form 6059B (Korean) (11/07)

미국세관 및 국경보호국(CBP)
미국에 오신 것을 환영합니다

미국세관 및 국경보호국은 미국이 금지하는 품목들이 불법으로 반입되는 것으로부터 미국을 보호하는 책임이 있습니다. CBP 의 직원은 귀하들을 심문하고 귀하의 개인 소지품을 감사할 권한이 있습니다. 만약 귀하께서 심문 대상으로 선택되신 경우, 반드시 예의 바르고 프로페셔널하며, 품위있는 대우를 받으시게 됩니다. CBP 의 감독자와 승객 서비스 담당자는 귀하의 질문에 응답해 드릴 것입니다. 의견 카드가 비치되어 있으니 칭찬의 말씀이나 피드백이 있으시면 이용해주 주십시오.

중요 정보

미국 거주자 — 해외에서 취득하고 미국으로 가지고 들어오는 모든 품목을 신고하십시오.

방문객 (비 거주자) — 미국에 남겨두실 모든 품목의 가치를 신고하십시오.

이 신고서에 **모든 품목을 신고**하고 품목의 가치를 미화 달러로 표시하십시오. 선물인 경우엔 소매 가격을 적으십시오.

관세 — CBP 직원이 관세를 결정할 것입니다. 미국 거주자는 일반적으로 휴대품에 대해 800 달러까지 면세액이 적용됩니다. 방문객(비 거주자)은 일반적으로 100 달러까지 면세가 적용됩니다. 관세금액은 면세액을 초과하는 최초의 1,000 달러에 대해 현행 세율을 이용해서 측정됩니다.

농산물 및 야생동물 제품—농산물 해충 및 금지된 야생동물의 미국 내 유입을 방지하기 위하여 다음 물품의 반입을 금지합니다: 과일, 채소, 식물, 식물제품, 흙, 육류, 육류제품, 조류, 달팽이, 기타 살아있는 동물 혹은 동물제품, 상기 물품을 미국세관 및 국경보호국 관원/세관 및 국경보호국 농산물 전문가/이류 및 야생동물 검사관에게 신고하지 않을 경우 벌금을 물게 되며, 물품 또한 압수될 수 있습니다.

규제 약물, 음란 외설물, 그리고 독극물은 일반적으로 반입이 금지됩니다. 농산물은 반입이 제한됩니다.

감사합니다. 미국에 오신 것을 환영합니다.

통화 또는 **화폐**의 운반은 금액의 고하를 막론하고 모두 합법적입니다. 하지만 10,000 달러 이상의 금액 (미화, 또는 동등한 가치의 외화, 또는 양자 합계)을 미국내로 반입 또는 미국외로 반출하실 때는 법에 의해 FinCEN 105 (예전의 'Customs Form 4790')를 작성하여 미국세관 및 국경보호국에 제출하셔야 합니다. 화폐에는 동전, 지폐, 여행자수표, 그리고 개인/은행, 자기앞수표, 주식, 채권과 같은 소지인에게 지불하는 증권이 포함됩니다. 타인이 귀하를 대신해서 통화나 화폐를 휴대하도록 한 경우라도 FinCEN 105 를 작성해서 신고하셔야 합니다. 휴대하시는 곳 금액을 신고하지 않으시면 통화나 화폐를 모두 몰수당하는 결과를 초래할 수 있으며, 귀하도 민사 처벌 및/또는 형사 소송을 당할 수 있습니다. 상기 중요한 정보를 자세히 읽으시고 사실대로 신고하신 후에 이 양식의 반대 쪽에 서명하십시오.

물품 설명

(공간이 부족하면 CBP Form 6059B 한 장을 더 사용해서 계속하십시오)	가치	CBP 용

합계

CBP Form 6059B (Korean) (11/07)

2. 대한민국 세관신고서(국문)

◎ 유의사항

모든 입국자는 신고서를 작성하여야 하며, 세관공무원이 지정하는 경우에는 휴대품 검사를 받으셔야 합니다.

◇ 허위신고하거나 불성실하게 신고할 경우 **관세법**에 의거 **5년** 이하의 **징역**에 처해지거나, 납부세액의 30%에 상당하는 **가산세**가 부과됩니다.

◇ **총포, 도검** 및 **테러물품**이 반입되지 않도록 휴대품 신고 및 신변검색에 협조하여 주시기 바랍니다.

◇ **타인의** 부탁으로 운반하는 물품은 마약, 밀수품일 수 있으니 신고하여 주시기 바랍니다.

◇ 성실하게 신고하는 여행자는 세금을 사후에 **납부**할 수 있습니다.

◇ 해외여행 중 전염병, 가축질병 발생지역 등을 방문한 경우에는 신고하여 주시기 바랍니다.

※ 휴대품 신고 및 면세제도에 의문이 있으면 **세관공무원** 및 **관세고객지원팀**(☎국번없이 1577-8577)으로 문의하십시오.

밀수신고는 국번없이 *125*

여행자(승무원) 세관 신고서

성 명		직 업	
주민등록번호		—	

여행목적 □관광 □사업 □친지방문 □공무 □교육 □기타

| 항공편명 | | 여행기간 | 일 |

한국에 입국하기 전에 방문했던 국가(총   개국)
1.   2.   3.   4.

한국내 주소(거소) :

전화번호 : ☎(   )

※ 가족여행인 경우에는 대표로 1인이 신고 가능 (동반가족수   명)

이 신고서 기재내용은 사실과 같습니다.

년   월   일

신고인 :   (서명)

세관신고 사항

[1] 다음 물품을 가지고 있습니까?

▶ 해당 □에 "V"표시를 하여 주시기 바랍니다.   있음 없음

① 총포·도검 등 무기류, 실탄 및 화약류, 유독성 또는 방사성 물질, 감청설비   □ □

② 아편·헤로인·코카인·대마 등 마약류   □ □

③ 미화 1만불 상당을 초과하는 외화, 원화, 유가증권 등(총 금액 : 약 _____)   □ □

④ 동·식물, 축산물, 과일·채소류 등   □ □

⑤ 멸종위기에 처한 야생동식물 및 관련 제품 (호랑이, 코브라, 악어, 산호, 웅담, 사향 등)   □ □

⑥ 위조상표 부착물품 등 지적재산권 침해물품   □ □

⑦ 위조지폐 및 위·변조된 유가증권   □ □

⑧ 판매 목적으로 반입하는 물품, 회사용품   □ □

⑨ 휴대품 면세범위("우측면 참조")를 초과한 물품   □ □

⑩ 다른 사람의 부탁으로 대리 운반하는 물품   □ □

[2] 해외(국내외 면세점 포함)에서 취득하거나 구입하여 휴대 반입하는 물품이 있는 경우에는 아래 표에 기재하여 주십시오. 단, 면세범위를 초과하지 않는 경우에는 기재하지 마시고, 면세범위를 초과하는 경우에는 "전체 물품내역"을 기재하여 주십시오.

① 주류·담배·향수

주 류	( )병, 총 ( )ℓ, 금액 ( )US$
담 배	( )갑(20개비 기준) 향수 ( )㎖

‣ 면세범위
- 일반여행자 : 주류 1병(1ℓ 이하로서 US$400이하), 담배 200개비, 향수 60㎖
  단, 만19세 미만인 경우 주류, 담배는 제외
- 승 무 원 : 담배 200개비

② 주류·담배·향수 이외의 물품

물 품 명	수 량	금 액
합 계		

‣ 면세범위
- 일반여행자 : US$400이하(자가사용, 선물용, 신변용품 등에 한함)
  ● 단, 농림축수산물, 한약재 등은 10만원 이하로서 품목별 수량 또는 중량에 제한이 있음
- 승 무 원 : US$100이하(품목당 1개 또는 1조에 한함)

대한민국 세관신고서(영문)

◎ Important information

All arriving people must complete this declaration and go through inspection if customs officers request.

◇ False or fraudulent declaration will result in a jail term of up to five years or an additional duty of 30% of the tax payable amount.

◇ Thank you for your cooperation in customs inspection or body-search to identify firearms, knives and terrorist materials prohibited to be carried in.

◇ Goods carried for other people could be narcotics, or smuggled effects. Please make sure to declare them.

◇ Please, report if you have visited areas affected by contagious or animal diseases during your stay abroad.

※ Please ask a customs officer or Customs Customer Service Team (☎1577-8577) for more information on Customs declaration.

Call **125** for smuggling report

Passenger(Crew) Customs Declaration

Name			
Date of Birth (yyyy/mm/dd)		Passport No.	
Nationality	Occupation		Sex □Male □Female
Purpose of Travel	□ Sightseeing □ Official Duties	□ Business □ Study	□ Visiting Friends □ Others
Flight No.		Stay Period	Days

Countries visited prior to entry to Korea(Total: ___ countries)

1.　　　　2.　　　　3.　　　　4.

Address in Korea :

Tel. No. : ☎ (　　)

※ Only one written declaration is required per family
(Number of accompanying family members :　　persons)

I have made a correct and truthful declaration.

Date(yyyy/mm/dd)

Name　　　　　　　(Signature)

Customs Declaration

[1] Are you bringing with you?

※ Mark a "V" in the Yes or No box.

	Yes	No
① Firearms, knives, and other weapons, explosives, bullets, poisonous/ radioactive substances, monitoring facilities	□	□
② Illicit drugs such as opium, heroin, cocaine and cannabis	□	□
③ More than US$10,000, or equivalent in Korean or foreign currency, securities, etc. (Total amount : approx. _____)	□	□
④ Animals, plants, livestock products, fruits, vegetables, etc.	□	□
⑤ Internationally protected endangered animals, plants, or relevant products (tigers, cobras, crocodiles, coral, bear's gall, musk, etc.)	□	□
⑥ Fake goods or other item that infringes Intellectual Property Right	□	□
⑦ Counterfeit currency, notes or securities	□	□
⑧ Commercial goods for sale and corporate goods	□	□
⑨ Goods exceeding duty-free allowance(refer to the right)	□	□
⑩ Goods which you are asked to carry by other people	□	□

---

[2] Please complete this form if you carry in items acquired or purchased overseas including at domestic and foreign duty-free shops.
Do not fill in the form if the total amount or value of the goods is within the duty-free allowance.
Otherwise, please list details of the entire goods.

① Liquors, cigarettes, perfume

Liquors	(　)bottles, (　)ℓ in total, Value(US$) (　　)
Cigarettes	(　) packs(of 20 cigarettes)
Perfume	(　) mℓ

☞ Duty-free allowance
- Passengers: One bottle (1ℓ or less and valued at US$400 or less) of liquor, 200 cigarettes, and 60mℓ of perfume.
However, Minors (under 19yrs) are not allowed to bring in any liquor or cigarette.
- Crew: 200 cigarettes

② Items other than liquors, cigarettes, perfume

Item	Quantity	Value
Total		

☞ Duty-free allowance
- Passengers: Items whose combined value is US$400 or less
(However, the items should be for personal use or present)
* Note, agricultural·forestry·livestock·fishery products, herbal medicines or its materials valued at KRW100,000 or less may be entered duty-free, yet subject to item-specific quantity or weight limit.
- Crew: Items whose combined value is US$100 or less
(single or a set of article per item)

6) Entering the United States of America(미국 입국)

Embarkation & Disembarkation card / Tourist

Dialogue ❶
F : Flight attendant / P : Passenger

P : Excuse me. Do I have to fill this out?

F : Are you a U.S. citizen or a resident, ma'am?

P : No, I'm a Korean.

F : You will need to fill out this card. Would you like me to help you?

P : No, I don't think so.

F : Alright, ma'am. Have a nice trip.

Immigrant

Dialogue ❷
F : Flight attendant / P : Passenger

P : Excuse me. I live in the USA, but I'm not a citizen yet. Do I need to fill these cards out?

F : May I ask whether you have an immigrant visa, sir?

P : Yes, I have an immigrant visa.

F : Then you only have to fill out the customs declaration form, sir.

Customs Declaration card / Resident, citizen, tourist

Dialogue ❸

F : Flight attendant / P : Passenger

P : Do I need to fill out this card?

F : Yes, sir. All passengers must fill out the customs declaration card.

Notes

- resident : 거주자, 거주민
- immigrant : 이민자, 이주자
- whether ~(or not) : ~인지 아닌지
- only have to ~ : ~하기만 하면 된다.

● 참고자료

1. I-94(미국 입·출국 신고서)

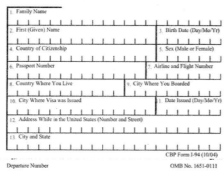

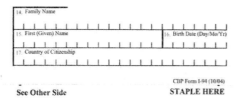

1. 성
2. 이름
3. 생년월일 (일/월/년도 순서)
4. 현재 거주국가
5. 남자: MALE/여자: FEMALE
6. 여권번호
7. 비행기 번호
8. 거주 국가
9. 탑승한 도시
10. 비자를 발급받은 도시
11. 비자를 발급받은 날짜
12. 미국에 거주할 곳 주소
13. 미국에 거주할 곳 도시, 주
14. 성
15. 이름
16. 생년월일
17. 국적

2. I-94W (미국 입. 출국 신고서: 비자 면제대상 승객)

DEPARTMENT OF HOMELAND SECURITY
U.S. Customs and Border Protection   OMB No. 1651-0113

Welcome to the United States
I-94W Nonimmigrant Visa Waiver Arrival/Departure Form
Instructions

This form is to be completed by every nonimmigrant visitor not in possession of a visitor's visa, who is a national of one of the countries enumerated in 8 CFR 217. The airline can provide your with the current list of eligible countries.

Type or print legibly with pen in ALL CAPITAL LETTERS. **USE ENGLISH**

This form is in two parts. Please complete both the Arrival Record, items 1 through 11 and the Departure Record, items 14 through 17. The reverse side of this form must be signed and dated. Children under the age of fourteen must have their form signed by a parent/guardian.

Item 7 - If you are entering the United States by land, enter LAND in this space. If you are entering the United States by ship, enter SEA in this space.

Admission Number

998957457 09

Arrival Record

VISA WAIVER

1. Family Name

2. First (Given) Name   3. Birth Date (day/mo/yr)

4. Country of Citizenship   5. Sex (male or female)

6. Passport Number   7. Airline and Flight Number

8. Country Where You Live   9. City Where You Boarded

10. Address While in the United States (Number and Street)

11. City and State

Government Use Only

12.   13.

CBP Form I-94W (10/04)

Departure Number   OMB No. 1651-0113

998957457 09

DEPARTMENT OF HOMELAND SECURITY
U.S. Customs and Border Protection
VISA WAIVER

14. Family Name

15. First (Given) Name   16. Birth Date (day/mo/yr)

17. Country of Citizenship

CBP Form I-94W (10/04)

See Other Side   **Staple Here**

Do any of the following apply to you? *(Answer Yes or No)*

A. Do you have a communicable disease; physical or mental disorder; or are you a drug abuser or addict?   ☐ Yes ☐ No

B. Have you ever been arrested or convicted for an offense or crime involving moral turpitude or a violation related to a controlled substance; or been arrested or convicted for two or more offenses for which the aggregate sentence to confinement was five years or more; or been a controlled substance trafficker; or are you seeking entry to engage in criminal or immoral activities?   ☐ Yes ☐ No

C. Have you ever been or are you now involved in espionage or sabotage; or in terrorist activities; or genocide; or between 1933 and 1945 were involved, in any way, in persecutions associated with Nazi Germany or its allies?   ☐ Yes ☐ No

D. Are you seeking to work in the U.S.; or have ever been excluded and deported; or been previously removed from the United States; or procured or attempted to procure a visa or entry into the U.S. by fraud or misrepresentation?   ☐ Yes ☐ No

E. Have you ever detained, retained or withheld custody of a child from a U.S. citizen granted custody of the child?   ☐ Yes ☐ No

F. Have you ever been denied a U.S. visa or entry into the U.S. or had a U.S. visa cancelled? If yes,
when? _____ where? _____   ☐ Yes ☐ No

G. Have you ever asserted immunity from prosecution?   ☐ Yes ☐ No

IMPORTANT: If you answered "Yes" to any of the above, please contact the American Embassy **BEFORE** you travel to the U.S. since you may be refused admission into the United States.

Family Name (Please Print)   First Name

Country of Citizenship   Date of Birth

WAIVER OF RIGHTS: I hereby waive any rights to review or appeal of a U.S. Customs and Border Protection officer's determination as to my admissibility, or to contest, other than on the basis of an application for asylum, any action in deportation.

CERTIFICATION: I certify that I have read and understand all the questions and statements on this form. The answers I have furnished are true and correct to the best of my knowledge and belief.

Signature   Date

Public Reporting Burden - The burden for this collection is computed as follows: (1) Learning about the form 2 minutes; (2) completing the form 4 minutes for an estimated average of 6 minutes per response. Comments concerning the accuracy of this burden estimate and suggestions for reducing this burden should be directed to U.S. Customs and Border Protection, Information Services Branch, Washington, DC 20229 and the Office of Management and Budget, Paperwork Reduction Project, OMB No. (1651-0113), Washington, DC 20503.

Departure Record
Important - Retain this permit in your possession; you must surrender it when you leave the U.S. Failure to do so may delay your entry into the U.S. in the future.
You are authorized to stay in the U.S. only until the date written on this form. To remain past this date, without permission from Department of Homeland Security authorities, is a violation of the law.
Surrender this permit when you leave the U.S.:
 - By sea or air, to the transportation line;
 - Across the Canadian border, to a Canadian Official;
 - Across the Mexican border, to a U.S. Official.
Warning: You may not accept unauthorized employment; or attend school; or represent the foreign information media during your visit under this program. You are authorized to stay in the U.S. for 90 days or less. You may not apply for: 1) a change of nonimmigrant status; 2) adjustment of status to temporary or permanent resident, unless eligible under section 201(b) of the INA; or 3) an extension of stay. Violation of these terms will subject you to deportation. Any previous violation of this program, including having previously overstayed on this program without proper DHS authorization, will result in a finding of inadmissibility as outlined in Section 217 of the Immigration and Nationality Act.
Port:

Date:

Carrier:

Flight # / Ship Name:

7. Landing and Deplaning(착륙과 승객 하기)

일반적으로 기장의 착륙 안내방송 후에 승무원이 착륙 안내 방송을 실시 한다. 착륙준비업무는 항공기 착륙 전에 담당 구역(zone)별로 이어폰, 잡지 등 객실에 비치된 물품을 회수하고 정 위치에 보관하고, 승객의 좌석 주변, 베게, 모포의 정리, 화장실의 승객 사용 여부를 확인하고 정리정돈을 한다. 승객으로부터 보관을 의뢰 받은 물품을 반환하고 승객의 착륙준비를 점검한다.

무엇보다 승객의 안전에 관련된 점검사항이 가장 중요하다. 승객의 착석, 좌석벨트 착용상태를 점검하고 좌석 등받이 및 테이블, 팔걸이, 발 받침을 정 위치에 둔다. 승객의 휴대 수하물 및 유동 물건의 고정을 확인하고 비상구 근처 및 통로의 정리상태를 확인한다. 전자기기의 사용 금지를 안내하고 객실 내의 시설물 안전 상태를 점검하고 유동물을 재확인한다. 마지막으로 객실 조명을 조절한다.

Words & Phrases

- deplaning : 하기
- We'll be landing shortly. : 곧 착륙하겠습니다.
- recline : 젖히다, 기대다.
- close/fold the tray table : 테이블을 접다
  ↔ open/unfold the tray table
- farewell
  = goodbye(작별인사)
- collection : 회수
  ↔ distribution (배포)
- I'm glad to hear that. : 그러시다니 다행입니다.
- block : 가로막다, 방해하다
- Thank you for flying with us. 저희 항공사를 이용해 주셔서 감사합니다.

1) Earphone Set Collection(이어폰 회수)

Dialogue ❶

F : Flight attendant / P : Passenger

F : Excuse me, sir. May I have your earphone set, please?

   We'll be landing shortly. Thank you, sir.

   Did you have a nice flight, sir?

P : Yes, I did.

F : I'm glad to hear that. How long are you going to be in Korea?

2) Seat Belt / Tray Table / Seat Back Situations
(안전벨트 / 테이블 / 좌석등받이 위치)

Seat belt

Dialogue ❶

F : Flight attendant / P : Passenger

F : Excuse me, sir. Would you mind fastening your seatbelt, please?

   We'll be landing soon. Thank you, sir.

Seat belt, mother and child

Dialogue ❷

F : Flight attendant / P : Passenger

F : Excuse me, ma'am. If you hold your baby outside the seat belt, it will be safer and more comfortable.

P : Oh, I see. Thanks.

F : My pleasure. Did you have a nice flight?

Seat back in reclined position / Tray table open

Dialogue ❸

F : Flight attendant / P : Passenger

F : Excuse me, ma'am. Would you mind returning your seat back to the upright position and closing your tray table, please? We'll be landing soon.

P : Alright.

F : Thank you, ma'am. Did you enjoy the flight?

P : Yes, I did.

F : I'm glad to hear that.

> **Notes**
>
> • hold : 안다. 들다.
> • seat back : 좌석 등받이
> • the upright position : 똑바로 선 위치
> • return the seat back to the upright position : 좌석 등받이를 똑바로 세우다

3) Passenger in the Aisle Prior to Landing
(착륙을 위해 통로에 있는 승객의 착석 유도)

Dialogue ❶

F : Flight attendant / P : Passenger

F : Excuse me, sir. Would you please return to your seat and fasten your seat belt? We'll be landing shortly.

> **Notes**
>
> • prior to
> = before(~전에)

4) Baggage Problems(승객 수하물 보관)

On the seat

Dialogue ❶

F : Flight attendant / P : Passenger

F : Excuse me, ma'am. Would you mind keeping your bag under the seat, please? It might fall off during landing. Thank you.

In the aisle / Blocking exits

Dialogue ❷

F : Flight attendant / P : Passenger

F : Excuse me. Is this bag yours?

P : Yes. Why?

F : Would you mind keeping your bag under the seat in front of you, please? We must keep the aisle clear, ma'am. We'll be landing shortly.

Notes

- might fall off : 떨어질 수도 있다. 떨어질지도 모른다
- block : 가로막다, 봉쇄하다.
- keep the aisle clear : 통로를 비워두다

5) Collecting Cups(컵 회수)

Dialogue ❶

F : Flight attendant / P : Passenger

F : Excuse me, ma'am. Have you finished with your drink?

P : Yes, I have.

F : May I take your cup, please? Thank you, ma'am.

We'll be landing shortly. Would you mind fastening your seat belt and closing your tray table?

Notes

collect : 모으다. 회수하다.

6) Deplaning and Farewell(하기와 작별)

Saying good bye

Dialogue ❶

F : Flight attendant / P : Passenger

F : Good bye. Thank you for flying with us. See you again.

Dialogue ❷

F : Flight attendant / P : Passenger

F : How was your flight?

P : It was wonderful. Thank you.

F : Would you make comments on us so our service can be improved?

P : Everything was fine.

F : Thank you. I hope to see you again soon.
Thank you for flying with Asiana Airlines. Have a nice day.

OR

Thank you for being with us today.

Helping a passenger

Dialogue ❸

F : Flight attendant / P : Passenger

F : May I help you with your bags, ma'am?

P : No, thank you. I can handle them.

F : All right. Thank you for flying with us. Good bye.
See you again.

Notes

- make comments on : ~에 관해 언급하다
- so(that) ~ : ~할 수 있도록
- improve : 개선하다

Review Test

1. Write the meaning of the following words.

1) immigration _____

2) quarantine _____

3) embark _____

4) customs declaration _____

5) transit _____

6) immigrant _____

7) deplaning _____

8) recline _____

9) prior to _____

10) improve _____

2. Complete the sentences with the correct words. Change the word form if necessary.

was told	whether	only have to	for	going to
disembarkation card				

1) Thank you _____ flying with us. See you again.

2) Foreigners entering Korea must fill out the _____ .

3) Then you _____ fill out the customs declaration form.

4) May I ask _____ you have an immigrant visa, sir?

5) How long are you _____ stay in Korea?

6) I'll be in Korea overnight, and I _____ I didn't need a visa.

3. Fill in the blank(s) with suitable word(s).

1) All passengers must _____ both sides of the card.

2) Would you _____ fastening your seatbelt, please?

3) Would you _____ returning your seat back to the _____ _____ ?

4) It _____ fall off during landing.

5) Would you make comments on us _____ our service can be improved?

4. Translate the following into English.

1) (카드) 작성하시는 것을 도와드릴까요?

   _____.

2) 곧 착륙하겠습니다.

   _____.

3) 우리는 통로를 비워두어야 합니다.

   _____.

4) 좌석 등받이를 똑바로 세워주시겠습니까?

   _____.

● 참고자료

1. 다양한 음료

VARIOUS BEVERAGE		
Cold Beverage	Mineral Water	
	Juice	· Orange Juice · Tomato Juice · Pineapple Juice · Apple Juice
	Soft Drink	· Cock / Diet Cock · Sprite / Diet Sprite
	Mixer류	· Tonic Water · Soda Water · Gingerale
Hot Beverage	Coffee	· Brew Coffee · Instant Coffee · Decaffeinated Coffee · Espresso Coffee
	Tea	· Black Tea · Green Tea · Ginseng Tea
Alcoholic Beverage	Still Wine	· Red Wine · White Wine
	Sparkling Wine	· Champagne
	Aromatized Wine	· Dry Vermouth
	Fortified Wine	· Sherry Wine · Port Wine
	Scotch Whisky	A whiskey distilled in Scotland from malted barley. (ex: Malt: Glenfiddich, Blended: Chivas Regal, Johnnie Walker Black)
	Bourbon Whisky (American Whisky)	A whiskey distilled from a fermented mash containing not less than 51 percent corn in addition to malt and rye. American whiskey made by distilling fermented maize mash.(ex: Jim Beam, Jack Daniel's)
	Canadian Whiskey	Made only in Canada, this distilled blend of rye, corn, wheat and barley is smoother and lighter than its cousins, rye whiskey and bourbon. It's wood-aged a minimum of 3 years with an average of 4 to 6 years.(ex: Canadian Club)
	Irish Whiskey	Whiskey made by the distillation of barley. Irish whiskeys are triple-distilled for extra smoothness and are aged in casks for a minimum of 4 (usually 7 to 8) years.(ex: Middleton)

Alcoholic Beverage	Brandy	A strong alcoholic drink made from wine (ex: Remy Martine V.S.O.P)
	Liqueur	A **liqueur** is a sweet alcoholic beverage, often flavored with fruits, herbs, spices, flowers, seeds, roots, plants, barks, and sometimes cream. The word liqueur comes from the Latin word *liquifacere* which means "to dissolve." This refers to the dissolving of the flavorings used to make the liqueur. Liqueurs are not usually aged for long periods, but may have resting periods during their production to allow flavors to marry. (ex: Baileys, Cointreau)
	Campari	Campari is an alcoholic aperitif obtained from the infusion of sixty ingredients, combined and macerated in a blend of distilled water and alcohol for a couple of weeks.
	Rum	Rum is a distilled beverage made from sugarcane by-products such as molasses and sugarcane juice by a process of fermentation and distillation. The distillate, a clear liquid, is then usually aged in oak and other barrels. (ex: Barcardi)
	Gin	A strong colorless alcoholic beverage made by distilling or redistilling rye or other grain spirits and adding juniper berries or aromatics such as anise, caraway seeds, or angelica root as flavoring. (ex: Beefeater)
	Vodka	Vodka is one of the world's most popular distilled beverages. It is a clear liquid containing water and ethanol purified by distillation from a fermented substance such as potatoes, grain or sugar beet molasses, and an insignificant amount of other substances: impurities and possibly flavourings. Vodka usually has an alcohol content of 35% to 50% by volume. (ex: Stolichnaya)
	Beer	Beer is the world's oldest and most popular alcoholic beverage. Some of the earliest known writings refer to the production and distribution of beer.[citation needed] It is produced by the fermentation of sugars derived from starch-based material the most common being malted barley; however, wheat, corn, and rice are also widely used, usually in conjunction with barley.

2. 특별음식

Special Meals	
Soft Bland Diet(SBDT)	무자극으로 위염, 위궤양 환자용 식사
Diabetic Meal(DBML)	당뇨병 환자용 식사
Low Cholesterol/Low Fat(LFML)	저콜레스테롤, 저지방, 심장질환, 동맥경화 등 성인병 환자용 식사
Soft Bland Diet(SBDT)	무자극으로 위염, 위궤양 환자용 식사
Diabetic Meal(DBML)	당뇨병 환자용 식사
Low Cholesterol/Low Fat(LFML)	저콜레스테롤, 저지방, 심장질환, 동맥경화 등 성인병 환자용 식사
No Dairy Products	우유가 들어가지 않는 우유분해효소가 없는 체질용 식사
Gluten Free(GFML)	글루텐이 들어가지 않으며 3세 이하의 내장질환 소아용 식사
Oriental Meal(ORML)	Chinese Style로 조리된 식사
Hindu Meal(HNML) : No Beef	쇠고기를 먹지 않는 힌두교도들을 위한 식사
Moslem Meal(MOML): No Pork	돼지고기를 먹지 않는 이슬람교도의 식사
Vegetarian Meal(VGML)	종교상, 건강상 또는 문화적 이유로 육류를 먹지 않는 채식주의자들의 식사
Kosher Meal(KSML)	유대정교 신봉자의 식사로 율법에 따라 조리한 식사로 돼지고기는 사용하지 않고 쇠고기, 양고기 등 기도를 올린 식사(닭고기나 생선과 Matzo라는 건빵으로 구성된 식사)
Infant Meal(IFML)	12개월 미만의 유아식으로 주로 우유 제공
Baby Meal(BBML)	12개월에서 24개월 정도의 유아식. 우유, 이유식 제공
Toddler Meal(TDML)	2세에서 6세 정도의 아동을 위한 식사. 씹고 삼키기 쉽게 조리
Child Meal	12세까지의 어린이용 식사로 어린이들이 선호하는 식단으로 구성

3. 칵테일 만들기

	Name	Base	Mixer
		Cocktail Recipe	
	Scotch Soda	Scotch Whisky 1Oz	Soda Water
Whisky Base Cocktail	Whisky Sour	Blended Whisky 1Oz	Lemon/Juice 0.3Oz
	Bourbon Cock	Bourbon Whisky 1Oz	Cock
	John Collins	Bourbon Whisky 1OZ	Lemon/Juice 0.3 Oz
	Gin Tonic	Gin 1 Oz	Tonic Water
Gin Base Cocktail	Gin Fizz	Gin 1 Oz	Lemon/Juice 0.3Oz / Soda Water
	Orange Blossom	Gin 1.5 Oz	Orange/Juice 1.5 Oz
	Tom Collins	Gin 1.5 Oz	Lemon/Juice 0.3 Oz
	Martini	Gin 1.5 Oz	Dry Vermouth
Vodka Base Cocktail	Vodka Tonic	Vodka 1 Oz	Tonic Water
	Bloody Mary	Vodka 1 Oz	Tomato/Juice
	Screw Driver	Vodka 1 Oz	Orange/Juice
Wine Base Cocktail	Kir	White Wine	Creme De Cassis
Champagne Base Cocktail	Mimosa	Champagne 1Oz	Orange/Juice Cointreau
	Kir Royal	Champagne	Cream De Cassis
	Buck Fizz	Champagne 2 Oz	Orange/Juice 2 Oz

4. 기내 메뉴

기내식을 포함한 데 고객 서비스 모든 분야에서 새롭고 우수한 품질을 인정받아
SKYTRAX 사 5 Star Airline 에 선정되었으며, 국제기내식협회 (ITCA)주관
'2006 Mercury Award' 기내식 부문 금상을 수상하였습니다.
고객 여러분의 많은 성원에 감사 드리며, 창립 20주년을 맞이한 저희 아시아나항공은
더욱 정성스러운 기내서비스를 위해 끊임 없는 노력을 기울이겠습니다.

We are proud to announce that SKYTRAX awarded 5 Star Airline ranking status
to Asiana Airlines, with service quality being singled out for distinction.
ITCA (International Travel Catering Association) has presented us the prestigious
'2006 Mercury Award' Gold in the Category 2, Food or Beverage.
To celebrate the 20th anniversary of the founding, we appreciate your support and
we will continue to make every effort to provide you with excellent service.

Menu
서울 - 뉴욕
Seoul - New York
2008. 12.

Seoul - New York

저녁식사

양식

전채
새우 샐러드

야채 샐러드
이탈리언 드레싱

쇠고기 안심 스테이크 378kcal
감자와 당근, 브로콜리

초콜릿 브라우니

차와 커피 *UCC*

한식

우엉&땅콩 조림과 계란말이

비빔밥 498kcal
죽, 김치

신선한 과일

차와 커피 *UCC*

Dinner

Western Style

Appetizer
Shrimp Salad

Mixed Salad
Italian Dressing

Beef Tenderloin Steak 378kcal
Potato, Carrot and Broccoli

Chocolate Brownies

Tea & Coffee *UCC*

Korean Style

Hard-boiled Burdock &
Peanut and Eggroll

Bi-Bim-Bab 498kcal
Steamed Rice, Assorted Vegetables
Soup and Kimchi

Fresh Fruit

Tea & Coffee *UCC*

晩 餐

西餐

前菜
虾沙拉

蔬菜沙拉
意大利式沙料

香煎牛扒 378kcal
土豆、胡萝卜与西兰花

巧克力布朗尼斯

茶与咖啡 *UCC*

韩餐

煮成牛蒡与花生、鸡蛋卷

拌饭 498kcal
汤、泡菜

新鲜水果

茶与咖啡 *UCC*

가벼운 식사

연어 샐러드

닭고기 요리 473kcal
백반, 땅콩, 당근

또는

농어 생선요리 345kcal
고추장 소스
백반

신선한 과일

차와 커피 *UCC*

Snack

Poached Salmon Salad

Deep Fried Chicken 473kcal
Steamed Rice, Nuts and Carrot

or

Poached Seabass 345kcal
Hot Pepper Paste Sauce
Steamed Rice

Fresh Fruit

Tea & Coffee *UCC*

点 心

三文鱼沙拉

红炸子鸡 473kcal
米饭、花生与胡萝卜

或

香煎鲈鱼 345kcal
辣椒酱汁
米饭

新鲜水果

茶与咖啡 *UCC*

● RA환경인증 커피 Rainforest Alliance Certified Coffee *UCC*
지구 환경보두 및 합대우입 유지 목저으로 설립된 국세적인 비영리 환경 난세민
RA인증을 받은 친환경 커피
This RA Coffee guarantees that coffee beans are produced using eco-friendly
methods.
本环保型咖啡豆是为了地球环境保护及热带雨林的维持为目的制的、并且被
国际性IⅡ热利环境机构RA 认可的。
손족 예상보다 많은 주문으로 인해 혹여나혼, 드리움 세공치지 못하게 될 때는 양해를 양해해주시고.

We apologize if your choice is not available due to unexpectedly high demand.

倘如 金阁要思不断的订食过量、而未能满足您的订餐要求、请联系见谅。

** 상기 식사에 대한 칼로리 계산은 식품 성분표, CAN pro software(한국영양학회의 영양 분석 프로그램) 및
USDA(미국 농무부)Nutrient Data Base를 이용하여 계산되었습니다.
** The above calories are calculated by using a Korean Food Composition Table,
CAN pro software (Computer Aided Nutritional Analysis developed by Korean
Nutrition Society) and USDA (United States Department of Agriculture) Nutrient
Data Base.
上面的关于计算的热量计算是使用食品成份表、韩国营养学会的营养分析软件、及美国农业部
营养部的有关资料分计算的。

▶ **American Culture 3**: 술집(Bar) 관련하여

미국에서 술집(Bar)에 가게 되면 술값을 지불하는 두 가지
방법이 있습니다. 하나는 'Pay cash'(현금지불)이고 또 다른
하나는 'Tab'을 사용하는 것입니다. Bar에 가면 종업원이
주문을 받기 전에 "Do you want to run a tab?"이라고
물어봅니다. 여기서 tab이란 바텐더(Bartender)가 손님의
크레디트 카드를 받아서 보관을 해두고 주문한 술을
손님의 크레디트 카드에 부과를 합니다. 술집을 떠날 때
청구서에 손님이 사인을 하면 그날 마신 술값이 모두
지불되는 방식입니다. Tab의 경우엔 손님들이 술을
마시다가 술값을 지불하지 않고 돌아가는 것을 방지하기
위한 수단입니다.

▶ **Grammar Note 3**: 셀수없는 명사의 양을 측정하고자 할 때

1. 물이나 우유는 액체이므로 그 양을 컵이나 유리컵에 담아야 그 양을 측정할 수
있습니다. 그 밖에 쌀. 설탕. 밀가루 등과 같이 셀 수 없는 명사들은 용기에 담아야만
그 양을 측정할 수 있습니다.

> 예 · I have a cup of coffee.
>   · She has a bag of rice

2. 몇 가지 예들

   ① a carton of eggs
   ② a glass/cup of green tea
   ③ a pound of meat
   ④ a can/bowl of soup
   ⑤ a slice/piece of bread
   ⑥ a glass/cup of orange juice
   ⑦ a glass of beer
   ⑧ a bunch of banana
   ⑨ a head of cabbage
   ⑩ a jar of jam

주의 두 잔의 커피라는 표현을 쓸 때에는 two cups of coffee 라고 해야 합니다.
   NOT two cups of coffees

3. a/an 셀 수 있는 하나의 명사 앞에 쓰입니다. 하지만, 셀 수 없는 명사 앞에는 붙일 수 없습니다.

예 · A money (X)

　· Much money (O)

　· I'd like an advice. (X)

　· I'd like some advice. (O)

주의 many 의 경우 셀 수 있는 명사가 복수 일 때 사용 합니다. 그러나, much 는 셀 수 없는 명사와 함께 쓰입니다. A lot of 는 셀 수 있는 명사와 셀 수 없는 명사 모두 사용할 수 있습니다.

Unit 04

Walk Around and Personal Touch
고객동향 파악 및 맞춤 서비스

1. Handling Sick Passengers(환자 서비스)

Words & Phrases

- airsick : 비행기 멀미가 나는
  → get airsick(비행기 멀미가 나다)
  airsick bag(멀미 봉투)
- nauseous
  = nauseated(메스꺼운, 토할 것 같은)
- vomit
  = throw up(토하다)
- take : (약을) 복용하다
  → take medicine
- anti-airsickness medicine : 비행기 멀미약
- pill : 알약(또는 알약을 세는 단위)
- for cabin crew use only : 객실 승무원 전용
- I hope you'll feel better. : 쾌유를 빕니다.

1) Sick Passenger(환자)

Dialogue ❶
F : Flight attendant / **P** : Passenger

P : Excuse me. I get airsick really easily.

- I feel nauseous / nauseated.

- I have indigestion / an upset stomach.

- I have heartburn.

- I have diarrhea.

Do you have anything for that?

- Do you have anything I can take?

- Do you have any medicine?

- Can I have some medicine, please?

F : Yes, we have some anti-airsickness medicine. Would that be alright, sir?

P : Yes, thanks.

F : Just a moment, sir, I'll bring it to you immediately.

(After a while)

F : Here is an anti-airsickness tablet and a glass of water.

P : Thank you very much.

F : You are welcome. I hope you feel better soon.

Notes

- indigestion : 소화불량, 체증
- upset stomach : 배탈
- heartburn : 속쓰림
- diarrhea : 설사
- feel better
  = get better(나아지다, 회복되다)
- tablet : 정제, 알약

2) Airsickness During the Flight(비행기 멀미 승객)

Dialogue ❶

F : Flight attendant / **P** : Passenger

P : Excuse me. I feel like vomiting.

  - I feel like throwing up.

  - I feel nauseous / nauseated.

F : Here is an airsick bag for you just in case you vomit, ma'am.

  Is there anything that I can do for you?

P : Do you have anything I can take?

F : Yes, but we have some medicine for cabin crew use only.

  It's called Bonaling-A which is the same medicine as the Dramamine.

  Would that be alright?

P : Yes, I'll have that.

F : Certainly, ma'am. Just a moment, please.

  (After a while)

  Here's your medicine.

P : Thanks a lot.

F : My pleasure. I hope you'll feel better.

  (After a while)

  How are you feeling, ma'am?

P : I feel better. Thanks.

F : You're welcome. I am glad to hear that.

  Can I get you anything else?

P : No, thanks.

• feel like ~ing : ~하고 싶은 생각이 들다. ~할 것 같다
• just in case : ~할 경우를 위해
• How are you feeling? : (기분이나 몸상태가) 좀 어떠십니까?

3) Sore Throat(인후염)

Dialogue ❶

F : Flight attendant / **P** : Passenger

P : Excuse me. The air in here is dry and my throat has become a little sore.
Do you have any medicine?

F : I'm sorry, sir. But I'm afraid we don't have anything for a sore throat.
Would you care for some hot tea with lemon?

P : Yes, please.

F : Certainly, sir. Just moment, please.

(After a while)

Here is your tea. I hope you'll feel better.

throat : 목구멍

have a sore throat : 목이 아프다, 목감기에 걸리다

　cf　 have a runny nose(콧물이 나다)

have a cough(기침이 나다)

have a cold in the nose(코감기에 걸리다)

have a frog in one's throat(목이 쉬다, 목이 잠기다)

4) Headache(두통)

Dialogue ❶

F : Flight attendant / **P** : Passenger

P : Excuse me. I have a headache.

Do you have any medicine?

F : Certainly, ma'am. Just a moment, please.

(After a while)

Here's some Tylenol. Please, take two pills with this water.

P : Thanks.

F : You're welcome. I hope you'll feel better.

have a headache : 머리가 아프다

　cf　 have a stomachache/toothache(배가/이가 아프다)

2. Service and Comfort(서비스와 각종 편의 제공)

Words & Phrases

- inexperienced : 미숙한, 익숙하지 않은
- ventilation : 통풍, 환기
- adjust : 조절하다, 조정하다
- recline the seat : (좌석을) 기울이다, 젖히다
- return the seat(back) to the upright position : 좌석을 바로세우다
- Have a nice rest. : 편히 쉬십시오.
- uncomfortable : 불편한
- blanket : 담요, 모포
- How about ~(명사/~ing) : ~는 어떠십니까?
  - How about some coffee or tea?
- be scheduled to : ~할 예정이다

1) Passenger Service Unit / Inexperienced Passenger
(승객 편의시설 / 비행기 시설에 익숙하지 않은 승객)

Ventilation

Dialogue ❶

F : Flight attendant / P : Passenger

P : Excuse me. How do I adjust the ventilation?

F : Please turn the knob, ma'am.

Volume control

Dialogue ❷

F : Flight attendant / P : Passenger

P : How do I adjust the volume?

F : Please turn this dial, sir.

OR

F : Please press these buttons to adjust, sir.

Channel selector

Dialogue ❸

F : Flight attendant / P : Passenger

P : Excuse me. How do I change channels?

F : Please turn this dial, ma'am.

OR

F : Please press these buttons to change, ma'am.

Light switch

Dialogue ❹

F : Flight attendant / P : Passenger

P : How do I turn on / off the light?

F : Please push the switch, sir.

OR

F : Please press the button on the unit.

Earphone jack

Dialogue ❺

F : Flight attendant / P : Passenger

P : Excuse me. Where do I plug in the earphone?

F : Right here. This one, sir.

Notes

· knob : 손잡이, 다이얼
  twist the knob to the left (손잡이를 왼쪽으로 돌리다)
  pull out the door knob (문 손잡이를 당기다)
· turn up/down the volume : 볼륨을 올리다/낮추다
  cf turn on/off the light
    = switch on/off the light (전등을 켜다/끄다)
· plug in : 플러그를 꽂다

2) Passenger Seat / Mechanical Instruction(좌석 작동설명)

Reclining seat

Dialogue ❶

F : Flight attendant / P : Passenger

P : How do I recline my seat?

F : Please press this button and lean back, sir.

Seat to upright position

Dialogue ❷

F : Flight attendant / P : Passenger

P : Excuse me. How do I return my seat to the upright position?

F : Please press this button and lean forward, ma'am.

- mechanical : 기계의, 기계로 작동하는
- instruction : 지시, 설명
- lean back : 뒤로 기대다, 뒤로 젖히다
  ↔ lean forward

3) Cabin Service(기내 서비스)

Passenger looks cold, Uncomfortable

Dialogue ❶

F : Flight attendant / P : Passenger

F : Would you like a blanket, ma'am?

P : Yes, please.

F : And here's a pillow.

Would you care for some hot tea or coffee, ma'am?

P : Yes, that would be nice. I want some hot tea.

F : Certainly, ma'am.

(After a while)

Here's your tea, ma'am. Have a nice rest.

Dialogue ❷

F : Flight attendant / P : Passenger

F : Would you like a blanket, sir?

P : Yes, please.

F : And here's a pillow.

Would you care for some hot tea or coffee, sir?

P : No, thanks.

F : Alright, sir. Have a nice rest.

Pillow request

Dialogue ❸

F : Flight attendant / **P** : Passenger

F : Would you like a pillow, ma'am?

P : Oh, sure.

F : Here's your pillow. Have a nice rest.

Would you care for some hot tea or coffee, ma'am?

OR

Can I get you anything else, ma'am? Hot tea or coffee?

Stretch out

Dialogue ❹

F : Flight attendant / **P** : Passenger

F : Excuse me, ma'am. Would you like to lie down?

We have empty rows in the middle of the cabin. Would that be alright, ma'am?

P : Oh, yes. Thank you.

F : This way, please. Here is your seat. Would you like a pillow and a blanket?

P : Yes, thank you.

F : You're welcome. Have a nice rest, ma'am.

Stretch out / Row unavailable

Dialogue ❺

F : Flight attendant / P : Passenger

P : Excuse me.

F : Yes, sir? Can I help you?

P : Do you have an empty row somewhere? I want to lie down.

F : I'm sorry, sir, but I'm afraid all the seats are occupied.
Would you care for something to drink, sir?

P : Yes, beer please.

F : Alright, sir. I'll get one for you soon.

(After a while)

Here is your beer. I'm Sorry again, sir.

Notes

- uncomfortable : 불편한
- stretch out : 몸을 뻗어 눕다
- lie down : 눕다
- empty row : 빈 줄/열

4) Bored Passenger(지루한 승객)

Newspaper service

Dialogue ❶

F : Flight attendant / P : Passenger

F : Are you enjoying the flight?

P : Yes... it's alright.

F : Would you care for a newspaper or a magazine?

P : Yes, please. Do you have Korea Herald?

F : Certainly, ma'am. Just a moment, please.

(After a while)

Here's the newspaper you requested, ma'am.

Drink service

Dialogue ❷

F : Flight attendant / **P** : Passenger

F : Are you enjoying the flight?

P : Well, it's alright.

F : Would you care for a newspaper or a magazine?

P : No, thank you.

F : How about some coffee or tea?

P : Do you have any apple juice?

F : Certainly, ma'am. Just a moment, please.

(After a while)

Here's your apple juice, ma'am.

Notes

• How about + 명사/ ~ing? : ~는 어떠십니까?(권유, 제안)

1. Write the meaning of the following words.

1) nauseous _____

2) vomit _____

3) anti-airsickness medicine _____

4) indigestion _____

5) upset stomach _____

6) have a sore throat _____

7) ventilation _____

8) knob _____

9) uncomfortable _____

10) stretch out _____

2. Complete the sentences with the correct words. Change the word form if necessary.

lie down	feel like	adjust	just in case	care for	turn

1) Here is an airsick bag for you _____ you vomit, ma'am.

2) How do I _____ the ventilation?

3) How do I _____ off the light?

4) Would you _____ some hot tea with lemon?

5) Excuse me. I _____ throwing up.

6) Do you have an empty row somewhere? I want to _____ .

3. Fill in the blank(s) with suitable word(s).

1) Here's some Tylenol. Please, _____ two pills.

2) **P** : How do I recline my seat?

   F : Please press this button and _____ _____ .

3) I hope you'll _____ better.

4) I'm sorry, but I'm _____ all the seats are occupied.

5) _____ _____ some coffee or tea?

4. Translate the following into English.

1) (기분이나 몸상태가) 좀 어떠십니까?

   _____.

2) 따뜻한 차나 커피를 가져다 드릴까요?

   _____.

3) 편히 쉬십시오.

   _____.

3. Walking-Around Service(고객동향 파악)

Words & Phrases

- New York is 14 hours behind Seoul. : 뉴욕은 서울보다 14시간 늦습니다.
- time difference
  = difference in time(시차)
  ex What's the time difference between Seoul and Chicago?
- It takes + 시간 + to ~ : ~하는데 …만큼 시간이 걸리다
  ex It takes about an hour to get to the airport.
    → How long does it take to ~ : ~하는데 얼마나 걸립니까?
- turbulence : 난기류
- make sure : 반드시/꼭 ~하다
- scheduled flight time : 예정 비행 시간
- Could you tell me ~ : ~를 알려주시겠습니까?
- How much is the bus fare? : 버스 요금은 얼마입니까?
- I recommend (that) you +동사원형 : ~하실 것을 권해드립니다

Local time

Dialogue ❶

F : Flight attendant / **P** : Passenger

P : Excuse me.

F : Yes, sir? May I help you?

P : What time is it in New York?

F : It's about 11 o'clock in the morning. New York is 14 hours behind Seoul.

P : Oh, thanks. Is it Monday or Sunday?

F : It's Sunday, sir.

P : What time are we arriving in New York?

F : We are scheduled to arrive at 2:30 pm, sir.

P : Thank you very much.

F : You are welcome. Have a pleasant flight, sir.

Flight time

Dialogue ❷

F : Flight attendant / P : Passenger

P : How long is it going to take us to get to Chicago?

F : Our scheduled flight time after take off will be 13 hours, ma'am.

P : What's the time difference between Seoul and Chicago?

F : Chicago is 15 hours behind Seoul, ma'am.

P : I see. Thank you.

F : You're welcome, ma'am.

Arrival time

Dialogue ❸

F : Flight attendant / P : Passenger

F : Excuse me. Would you care for some tea, sir?

P : Yes, please. Um... how long will it be before we get to LA?

F : We expect to arrive in about two and a half hours.

P : I see. Thanks.

F : My pleasure. Have a nice flight.

Passenger wants to take a service item

Dialogue ❹

F : Flight attendant / P : Passenger

P : Excuse me. Can I take this cup as a souvenir?

F : I'm sorry, but I'm afraid we have to use the cup for other flights, sir.

　　Would you like some Asiana playing cards or postcards instead, sir?

Severe turbulence

Dialogue ❺

F : Flight attendant / P : Passenger

P : Excuse me. Is this plane okay?

F : We are just having some turbulence. Don't worry, ma'am.
Please make sure your seat belt is fastened, ma'am.

Location of lavatory

Dialogue ❻

F : Flight attendant / P : Passenger

P : Excuse me. Could you tell me where the toilet is?

F : Certainly, ma'am. It's in the back of the cabin on your right, ma'am.
Would you like me to show you where it is?

P : No, thanks. I'll go myself.

F : Alright, ma'am.

Position of the aircraft

Dialogue ❼

F : Flight attendant / P : Passenger

P : Excuse me. Where are we flying over now?

F : Just a moment, please. I'll find out for you, sir.

(After a while)

Excuse me. We are flying over Jeju Island.

P : Oh, really? Is it part of Korea?

F : Yes, it is. It's on the southern coast.

Closing shades during the movie presentation
: Passenger wants to see the movie

Dialogue ❽

F : Flight attendant / P : Passenger

F : Excuse me. Would you mind if I close this shade?

P : No, I don't. Please go right ahead.

F : Thank you, sir.

I hope you enjoy the movie.

Closing shades during the movie presentation: Using reading light

Dialogue ❾

F : Flight attendant / P : Passenger

F : Excuse me. We'll be showing the movie shortly.

Would you mind closing your window shade, please?

P : I'm not going to watch the movie but I'm going to read.

F : Alright, ma'am. But I am afraid we have to close the window shades while

the movie is showing. Would you like me to turn on the reading light?

P : No, thanks. I'll do it. Where is it?

F : Please press the reading light button that looks like a light bulb.

Would you care for something to drink?

P : No, thank you.

F : Enjoy the flight, ma'am.

Waking up passenger

Dialogue ⑩

F : Flight attendant / P : Passenger

F : Good morning, sir. Did you have a nice rest?

Would you care for some fruit juice?

P : Oh, yes. Orange juice, please.

F : Certainly, sir. Just a moment, please.

Here is your orange juice. We'll be serving breakfast shortly.

Returning passengers's personal belongings: Clothing / Bag

Dialogue ⑪

F : Flight attendant / P : Passenger

F : Excuse me, ma'am. Here's your coat and bag.

We'll be landing in about 10 minutes.

P : Thank you.

F : You're welcome. Have a nice stay in Korea.

Returning passenger's personal belongings: Not sure of ownership

Dialogue ⑫

F : Flight attendant / P : Passenger

F : Excuse me, sir. This is your suitcase, isn't it?

We'll be landing in about 10 minutes.

P : Yes, thank you.

F : My pleasure. I hope you enjoyed our flight today.

Returning passenger's personal belongings
: Passenger requests for personal items

Dialogue ⑬

F : Flight attendant / **P** : Passenger

P : Excuse me. Would you bring me my bag I gave you earlier?

F : Certainly, ma'am. Just a moment, please.

(After a while)

Here's your bag, ma'am. Did you enjoy our flight today?

P : Yes, it was great. Thank you.

F : I'm glad to hear that. I hope to see you on board again.

Notes

- local time : 현지시각
- be scheduled to : ∼할 예정이다
- get to : ∼에 도착하다
- in about two and a half hours : 약 2시간 반 후에
- souvenir : 기념품
- fly over : ∼위를 날다. ∼상공을 지나다
- Would you mind if I ∼ : 제가 ∼해도 될까요?
  → (허락할 경우) 대답은 No, I don't. / Certainly not. / Go ahead, please. 등으로 함.
- close the shade : 차양을 닫다
- not A but B : A가 아니고 B임
- while + 주어 + 동사 : ∼하는 동안
  ㄹ during + 명사(∼중에, ∼하는 동안)
    during the flight
- light bulb : 전구
- belongings : (보통 복수형으로 쓰임) 소지품
- bring : 가져오다
  ㄹ take(가져가다)
- earlier : 전에, 아까

4. Destination City Information(목적지 도시 안내)

- destination : 행선지, 목적지
- transportation : 수송, 교통수단
  - traffic (교통, 교통량)
- What kind of transportation is available? : 어떤 교통수단이 있습니까?
- recommend : 추천하다
- retail shop : 소매점
- tourist desk : 관광안내 데스크
- shopping district : 쇼핑 지구/단지
- take a Limousine bus : 리무진 버스를 타다

1) Transportation from the Airport to the Destination
(공항에서 목적지까지의 교통수단)

Dialogue ❶

F : Flight attendant / **P** : Passenger

P : Excuse me. This is my first trip to Korea.

What kind of transportation is available from Incheon Airport to downtown?

F : Well, we have buses and taxies.

A taxi will cost about fifty thousand won, depending on the traffic. I recommend you to take a Limousine bus and it costs about ten thousand won and it's nonstop.

P : Thank you.

F : You're welcome. Have a nice stay in Korea.

Other destinations

Dialogue ❷

F : Flight attendant / P : Passenger

P : What's the arrival time in Incheon?

F : 6:40 in the morning, sir.

P : How long does it take to downtown Seoul from the airport?

F : It takes about one hour and a half by Limousine bus, depending on the traffic.

P : How much is the bus fare?

F : It's about ten thousand won, sir.

Notes

· from A to B : A에서 B까지
· cost : (비용이) 들다
· depend on : ～에 달려있다. ～에 좌우되다.
  → It depends.(경우에 따라 달라. 그야 모르지)
· take : (버스, 택시 등을) 타다. 이용하다
· by + 교통수단 : ～을 타고

2) Shopping Information(쇼핑정보)

Dialogue ❶

F : Flight attendant / P : Passenger

P : Do you know any good places for shopping in Seoul?

F : I would recommend Itaewon, Myung Dong and Namdaemun Market, ma'am.

There are department stores and many retail shops in Myung Dong.

Namdaemun Market is the biggest traditional market in Korea, and you can purchase various shopping items at an inexpensive price.

In Itaewon, you can get nice souvenirs, cheap clothes and shoes. Moreover, the shopkeepers speak English.

For more information, please go to the tourist desk on the first floor of the terminal building. They'll be glad to help you, ma'am.

Notes

- good places for : ~하기 좋은 곳
- inexpensive
  = cheap(저렴한)
- shopkeeper : 상점 주인, 상인
- terminal building : 공항청사
- be glad to help : 기꺼이 돕다

3) Hotel Information(호텔정보)

Dialogue ❶

F : Flight attendant / **P** : Passenger

P : Could you recommend any hotels in Seoul?

This is my first trip to Korea and I don't know any places to stay.

F : Well, I recommend the Hyatt Hotel. It is very good but expensive.

For a cheaper hotel, I would like to recommend Hamilton Hotel in Itaewon. It's in the Itaewon shopping district.

But for more information, please go to the hotel information desk on the first floor of the terminal. They'll help you to find good accommodations, sir. Have a nice stay in Korea.

- for a cheaper hotel : 더 저렴한 호텔로는
- accommodations : 숙박시설

4) Money Exchange Information(환전정보)

Dialogue ❶

F : Flight attendant / **P** : Passenger

P : Excuse me. I have to change some money. Is there a bank in the terminal building?

F : Yes, sir. The bank is on your left after you leave the customs area.

P : Can you tell me the exchange rate for dollars?

F : Well, I am not sure, but today's rate is about eleven hundred won to one US dollar.

P : Thank you.

F : You're welcome, sir. Have a nice stay in Korea.

- money exchange : 환전
- exchange rate : 환율

5. From Immigration To Customs(입국심사, 세관 안내)

Words & Phrases

- immigration : 입국심사
- customs (복수형으로 써서) 관세, 세관
  → customs area(세관 구역), customs declaration(세관 신고)
- What is the purpose of your visit? : 방문목적은 무엇입니까?
- claim the baggage : 짐을 찾다
- Which flight were you on? : 어느 항공편을 이용하셨습니까?
- fill out : (서류를) 기재하다, 작성하다
- Do you have anything to declare? : 신고할 물품은 없으십니까?
- What does your baggage look like? : 가방이 어떻게 생겼습니까?

1) Immigration(입국심사)

Dialogue ❶

O : Officer / **P** : Passenger

O : Good evening. May I see your passport?

P : Yes, here you are.

O : What is the purpose of your visit?

P : Tour.

O : How long do you intend to stay in Korea?

P : One month.

O : Where are you going to stay in Seoul?

P : Marriot Hotel.

O : All right, ma'am. Here is your passport and you may go now.

P : Thank you.

Notes

- intend to : ~할 작정이다
- may : (조동사) ~해도 좋다(허락)
  - ↔ may not(~해서는 안된다)

2) Baggage(수하물)

Claim

Dialogue ❶

A : Airline agent   / **P** : Passenger

P : Excuse me. Where can I claim my baggage?

A : Downstairs. Take that escalator, sir.

P : Thank you.

A : No problem.

Lost

Dialogue ❷

A : Airline agent   / **P** : Passenger

P : Excuse me. I cannot find my bags.

A : Which flight were you on?

P : Singapore Airlines Flight 700.

A : What do your baggages look like?

B : They are suitcases with red color.

A : Please show me your baggage claim tag.

P : Here you are.

A : Let me check.

(After a while)

Unfortunately your baggages have been sent to another airport and they will arrive later today.

P : Oh, that's terrible.

A : We are very sorry about that. Could you fill out this form about the description of your baggages, the value of your baggages's contents and the address where you are staying?

P : O.K. Here it is.

A : We'll deliver your baggages there tonight.

Notes

- Where can I ~? : ~하는 곳은 어디입니까?
- baggage claim tag : 수하물 영수증
- unfortunately : 불행히도
- be sent to : ~로 보내지다
- description : 묘사. 기술
- content : 내용(물)

3) Customs(세관)

Dialogue ❶

O : Officer   /   P : Passenger

O : Can I see your customs declaration form, please?

P : Sure. Here it is.

O : Do you have anything to declare?

P : No, I have only my personal effects.

O : What do you have in your shopping bag?

P : Oh, they are chocolates for my niece.

O : O.K. You may go.

P : Thank you.

Notes

· declare : (세관에) 신고하다
  customs declaration form : 세관 신고서
· effects
  = items, goods(물품)

Review Test

1. Write the meaning of the following words.

   1) time difference _____

   2) souvenir _____

   3) turbulence _____

   4) shade _____

   5) belongings _____

   6) transportation _____

   7) destination _____

   8) recommend _____

   9) retail shop _____

   10) inexpensive _____

   11) accommodations _____

   12) description _____

2. Complete the sentences with the correct words. Change the word form if necessary.

make sure	while	close	claim	get to	over

   1) How long will it be before we _____ LA?

   2) Please _____ your seat belt is fastened, ma'am.

   3) We are flying _____ Jeju Island now.

   4) Would you mind _____ your window shade, please?

   5) I am afraid we have to close the window shade _____ the movie is showing.

   6) Where can I _____ my baggage?

3. Fill in the blank(s) with suitable word(s).

1) What kind of transportation is _____ from Incheon airport to downtown?

2) We expect to arrive _____ about two and a half hours.

3) We'll be _____ the movie shortly.

4) I'm not going to watch the movie _____ I'm going to read.

5) A taxi will cost about sixty thousand won, _____ on traffic.

6) Would you _____ me to turn on the reading light?

4. Translate the following into English.

1) 뉴욕은 서울보다 14시간 늦습니다.

   _____.

2) 어느 항공편을 이용하셨습니까?

   _____.

3) 오후 2시 30분에 도착할 예정입니다.

   _____.

4) 공항에 도착하는 데는 약 1시간 정도 걸립니다.

   _____.

5) 리무진 버스를 타실 것을 권해드립니다.

   _____.

6) 차양을 내려도 괜찮겠습니까?

   _____.

● 참고자료

1. 수하물 표

고객용 수하물표 Baggage Tag

고가품 및 파손되기 쉬운 물품에 대한 안내
Please take out and hand-carry any valuable and fragile items

노트북, 캠코더, 카메라, 휴대폰, 현금, 유가증권, 귀금속, 의약품, 열쇠, 중요 서류, 전자 제품 및 귀중품과 파손이 되기 쉬운 물품은 손님께서 직접 휴대하시고 비행기에 탑승하여 주시기 바랍니다. 위탁수하물로 부치시는 경우 상기 물품의 분실, 또는 손상 시 당사에서는 일체 책임지지 않습니다.
Laptop computers, VCRs, Cameras, Mobile phones, Cash, Stocks, Jewelry, Keys, Medicines and confidential documents or other valuable and fragile items should be carried on board. Asiana Airlines shall not be liable for Loss, Stolen or Damages caused by violations of this regulation.

통상적인 수하물 처리 과정에서 발생한 경미한 파손 사고에 대한 배상 불가 안내
Asiana Airlines is not liable for any minor damages in normal baggage handling

별도의 안전한 보관함에 넣지 않은 악기류와 스포츠용품, 일상적인 수하물 취급 과정에서 발생하는 경미한 긁힘, 얼룩, 바퀴나 손잡이 파손 혹은 스트랩 분실에 대해서는 책임을 지지 않으며 보상을 하지 않습니다.
Asiana Airlines shall not be liable for broken wheels, lost straps/handles and minor damages(scratches, dents, cuts and stains etc.) of checked baggage, musical instruments or sport gears resulted from normal baggage handling.

4G I.D. TAG(LR( ) _____)

VR CG3U6C   2/33

JFK   OZ

OZ 756844

유용한 *Tips*

▶ American Culture 4

실례합니다(Excuse me)

· 미국 생활을 하면서 참 많이 듣게 되는 말 중 하나가 "Excuse me"일 것입니다. 대다수의 미국인들은 다른 사람과 가까운 거리를 두고 지나칠 때 "실례합니다(Excuse me)"라고 미안함을 표현합니다. 역으로 상대방이 나의 진로를 방해할 경우에도 "Excuse me"라고 표현 합니다.

· 미국인들은 'Personal Space'라고 해서 상대방과 일정한 간격을 유지하는데 이는 우리나라에서 좀처럼 보기 힘든 광경입니다. 그래서 다른 사람과 가까운 거리를 두고 지나칠 때 "Excuse me"라고 미안함을 표현하는 것도 상대방의 'Personal Space'를 침범했다고 생각하기 때문입니다. 미국인들이 엘리베이터나 극장, 비행기에서 옆 사람이 파고들면 예민한 반응을 보이는 것 역시 'This is my personal space.'라는 인식의 한 예라고 할 수 있습니다.

▶ Grammar Note 4: 명령문(Imperative)

영어에서 '명령문'을 사용하는 경우

1. 방향이나 사용법을 설명할 때 사용합니다.
    예 · Turn right on 5th street.
    · Put the sentences into the correct order.

2. 명령을 할 때 사용합니다.
    예 · Do not run!

3. 충고나 조언을 할 때 사용합니다.
    예 · Take a deep breathe.
    · Don't think about the past.

4. 경고를 할 때 사용합니다.
    예 · Watch out!
    · Don't drop!

5. 요청을 할 때 사용합니다. 주로 please와 함께 씁니다.
    예 · Please open the door. or Open the door, please.

    주의 명령문의 경우 주어는 사용하지 않습니다.
    예 · Sit down. (○)
    · You sit down. (X)

Unit 05

In-Flight Announcements
기내 안내방송

1. Pre-Boarding Announcement(탑승전 안내방송)

Good afternoon (morning, evening) ladies and gentlemen.

This is the pre-boarding announcement for flight _____ to (destination).

We are now inviting those passengers with small children, and any passengers requiring special assistance, to begin boarding at this time. Please have your boarding pass and identification ready. Regular boarding will begin in approximately ten minutes time. Thank you.

Pre-Boarding Announcement

손님 여러분,

_____ 까지 가는 _____ 편의 탑승 안내방송 입니다.

유아 동반 승객, 어린이, 도움을 필요로 하는 승객은 지금부터 탑승해 주시기 바랍니다.

탑승권과 여권을 준비해 주시고, 일반승객들은 10분 후에 탑승을 시작하도록 하겠습니다.

감사합니다.

2. Departure Delayed(출발 지연 방송)

With New Departure Time

May I have your attention, please?

We are sorry to announce that / _____ Airlines Flight _____ bound for _____

/ will be delayed due to heavy snow (strong wind, heavy rain, dust, dense fog).

The new departure time will be _____ (AM.P.M). Thank you.

With New Departure Time

안내 말씀 드리겠습니다.

_____ 까지 가는 _____ 항공 _____ 편은 _____ 공항의 폭설(강풍, 폭우, 황사,

짙은안개)로 인해 출발이 / (예:정보다) 지연되고 있습니다.

출발시간은 (오전 · 오후) _____ 입니다. 이점 널리 양해해 주시기 바랍니다.

감사합니다.

Without New Arrival Time

May I have your attention, please?

We are sorry to / announce that _____ Airlines / Flight _____ bound for ____

will be delayed due to / strong wind(heavy snow, heavy rain, dust, dense fog).

Further information / will be announced as soon as possible.

Thank you.

Without New Arrival Time

안내 말씀 드리겠습니다.

_____ 까지 가는 _____ 항공 _____ 편은 _____ 공항의 강풍(폭설, 폭우, 황사, 짙은안개)으로 인해 출발이 / (예:정보다) 지연되고 있습니다.

정확한 출발 시간은 빠른 시간 내에 알려드리도록 하겠습니다. 이점 널리 양해하여 주시기 바랍니다.

감사합니다.

3. Flight Cancelled(결항 안내방송)

May I have your attention, please?

We are sorry to announce that _____ Airlines Flight _____ bound for _____

has been cancelled due to dense fog(heavy snow, heavy rain, strong winds,

technical problems, sick passenger).

Passengers, who want to make a reservation for another flight, please come to

the information counter. Thank you.

Departure Cancelled

안내 말씀 드리겠습니다.

_____ 까지 가는 _____ 항공 _____ 편은 _____ 공항의 짙은 안개(폭설, 폭우, 강풍, 기술상의 문제, 위중한 환자)로 인해 / 결항되었습니다.

승객 여러분, 다음 비행편을 확인해 주시기 바랍니다.

감사합니다.

4. In-Flight Announcement(비행중 안내방송)

Baggage Securing

Ladies and gentlemen,

This is Asian Airlines flight _____ / bound for _____ .

For your comfort and safety, please put your carry-on baggage / in the overhead bins or under the seat in front of you.

When you open the overhead bins, please be careful as the contents may fall out.

Thank you.

Baggage Securing

손님 여러분,

이 비행기는 _____ 까지 가는 아시안 항공 _____ 편입니다.

안전한 여행을 위해, 가지고 계신 짐은 / 앞 좌석 밑이나 선반 속에 보관해 주시기 바랍니다.

선반을 여실 때는 / 먼저 넣은 물건이 떨어지지 않도록 조심해 주십시오.

감사합니다.

Welcome Announcement

Good morning(OR afternoon / evening), / ladies and gentlemen.

Captain _____ and the entire crew / would like to welcome you aboard /

Asian Airlines flight _____ (FLT NO.) / bound for _____ (DESTINATION).

Our flight time will be _____ hour(s) and _____ minutes/ following take-off.

Please make sure / your seat belt is securely fastened.

And please return your seat back and tray table / to their upright position.

The use of electronic devices / including mobile phones are not allowed / during take-off and landing.

Smoking in the cabin and lavatories / is prohibited at all times / during the flight.

We're pleased / to have you on board today / and we'll do our very best / to serve you.

Thank you for flying with us.

손님 여러분, 안녕하십니까?
저희 아시안 항:공에 탑승해 주셔서 감:사합니다.
이 비행기는 _____ 까지 가는 아시안 항:공 _____ 편입니다.
_____ 기장과 _____ 명의 승무원은 여러분을 정성껏 모시겠습니다.
목적지인 _____ 공항까지의 비행시간은 _____ 시간 _____ 분으로 예:정하고 있습니다.

지금부터 안전을 위해 / 좌:석벨트를 매:셨는지 / 확인해 주십시오.
또한, 좌석 등받이와 테이블은 제자리로 해 주십시오.
항:공법에 따라 / 비행기 이:착륙시, / 휴대전:화를 포함한 / 모:든 전:자:제:품을 사:용하실 수 없:습니다.
그리고, / 화장실과 기내에서는 / 금:연해 주시기 바랍니다.
여행 중 도움이 필요하시면 언:제든지 저희 승무원을 불러 주십시오.
_____ 까지 편안한 여행이 되시기 바랍니다.
감:사합니다.

Safety Video Showing

Ladies and gentlemen, /

We'd like to familiarize you / with the safety features of this aircraft.

Please take a moment / to view the following video program.

Thank you.

Safety Video Showing

손님 여러분, /

지금부터 / 기내 안전에 관한 비디오를 상:영해 드리겠습니다.

앞쪽의(에) 화:면에 / 잠시 주:목해 주시기 바랍니다.

감:사합니다.

Delayed Departure

Ladies and gentlemen, / we'll be(or we're) delayed (we're waiting for) /

● Choose one

1. due to air traffic.
2. our turn to take off
3. aircraft documents.
4. the completion / of check-in procedures by passengers.
5. the unloading / of an absent passengers baggage.
6. the completion / of baggage(or cargo) loading.
7. the departure (or take off) clearance.
8. passengers / from a connecting flight.
9. the loading / of additional food(or service items)
10. due to snow removal on the runway.
11. due to aircraft maintenance of this aircraft.
12. due to a problem with Emergency Escape Slide.

1. We'll depart as soon as possible.
2. We'll depart in about _____ hour(s) and _____ minutes.

We appreciate your understanding and patience. Thank you.

Delayed Departure

안:내 말:씀 드리겠습니다.

1. 지금 저희 비행기는 / 이:착륙하는 비행기가 많:아
2. 지금, 비행기 이:륙 순:서를 기다리고 있어.
3. 지금, 비행기 출항 서류를 기다리고 있어.
4. 지금, 출국 수속 중인 / 손님을 기다리고 있어.
5. 지금, 탑승하지 않은 손님의(에) / 수하물을 내리고 있어.
6. 지금, 수하물(화:물) 탑재가 계:속되고 있어.
7. 저희 비행기는 / 관:제탑의(에) / 이륙 허가를 기다리고 있어.
8. 지금, 연결편 손님을 기다리고 있어.
9. 지금, 기내식(서:비스 물품) 탑제를 기다리고 있어.
10. 지금 저희 비행기는 / 이곳 _____ (국제) 공항의(에) 활주로 제설 작업으로,
11. 비행기 정비 관계로,
12. 지금 저희 비행기는 / 비:상탈출용 미끄럼대에 문:제가 생겨,

출발이 / (예:정보다) 지연되고 있습니다.

1. 잠:시:후:, 출발하겠으니, / 양해해 주시기 바랍니다.
2. 약 _____ 시간 _____ 분 후:, 출발하겠으니, / 양해해 주시기 바랍니다.

감:사합니다.

Take Off

Ladies and gentlemen, /

We'll be taking off shortly.

Please make sure / your seat belt is securely fastened.

Thank You.

Take Off

손님 여러분, /

저희 비행기는 / 곧 이륙하겠습니다.

좌:석벨트를 매:셨는지 / 다시 한번 확인해 주십시오.

감사합니다.

Seat Belt Sign Off

Ladies and gentlemen, /

Although the seat belt sign / has been turned off.

In case of sudden turbulence, / please keep your seat belt fastened / at all times during the flight.

When opening the overhead bins, / be careful as the contents may fall out.

You may now use CD Players and laptop computers.

For further information on the types of electronic devices allowed on board / please refer to the magazine in your seat pocket.

We'd like to remind you / that smoking is prohibited in the cabin / and lavatories.

Your cooperation is much appreciated.

Thank you.

Seat Belt Sign Off

손님 여러분, /

방금 / 좌:석벨트 착용 표시등이 꺼졌습니다.

그러나 기류변화로 비행기가 갑자기 흔들릴 수 있으니, / 자리에 앉아 계실 때는 / 항상 좌석벨트를 매 주시기 바랍니다.

아울러, / 선반 속의 물건을 꺼내실 때는 / 안에 있는 / 짐들이 떨어지지 않도록 / 조심해 주십시오.

지금부터, / CD플레이어나 노트북 등을 사용하실 수 있습니다.

사용하실 수 있는 전자제품에 대한 자세한 내용은 / 기내지를 참고하시기 바랍니다.

그리고, / 화장실과 기내에서는 / 금:연 입니다.

감:사합니다.

Duty-Free Sales

Ladies and gentlemen, /

In a few minutes, / we'll begin our sales of duty-free items.

If you'd like to purchase any items, /

(cart basis)

please let us know / as the duty-free sales cart passes by your seat.

(order basis)

Please fill out the order form / in your seat pocket and give it to your flight attendant.

We accept Korean won, U.S dollar, Japanese yen and credit card.

The duty-free allowances for(Country name) are / _____ liter of liquor(s), _____ carton(s) of cigarettes for (visitors / residents) and ounce(s) of perfume.

For your convenience, / we have a pre-order form / which will allow you to order items / and pick them up on your return flight.

For further information, please contract your flight attendants.

Thank you.

Duty-Free Sales

손님 여러분, /
저희 기내에서는 필요하신 분들을 위:해 / 다양한 면:세품을 저:렴한 가격에 판매하고 있습니다.
잠:시후:, / 면:세품 판매를 시작할 예:정이니 / 구입을 원:하시는 분께서는

Cart basis : 면세품 판매대가 지나갈 때 구입하시기 바랍니다.
Order basis : 좌석 앞 주머니 속의 면세품 주문서를 작성하시어 승무원에게 전달해 주시기 바랍니다.

면세품 구입 시, 지불하실 수 있는 화:폐는 한국 원, 미국 달러, 일본 엔 과 신용카드 입니다.
참고로, _____ 에 입국하시는 손님의(에) 면:세 허용량은 / 주류 _____ 병(또는 리터), 담:배 _____ 보루, 향수 _____ 온스 입니다.

탑재되지 않은 일부 품:목이나, / 면:세품을 미리 구입하실 분은 / 면:세품 예:약 주:문제를 / 이:용해 주십시오.

보다 자세한 내:용은 / 저희 승무원에게 문:의(문:이)해 주십시오.

감:사합니다.

Ladies and gentlemen,

For entering the United States, please have your entry documents ready.

All passengers except U.S. citizens, / U.S. green card holders, / Canadian citizens and U.S. immigrant Visa holders / must fill out the Arrival card.

U.S. customs form must be completed by all passengers.

Families traveling together / only need to fill out one customs form.

Passengers carrying more than ten thousand US dollars, or the equivalent in foreign currency / must declare that amount on the customs form.

Fruits, Plants, Seeds, or other food items should also be declared.

(Transit Flight)

Those passenger continuing on to (Name of City) or traveling with connecting flights are also required / to obtain a transit card after deplaning / and proceed to the transit area.

For security reasons, (By request of the local Authorities,) please take all your belolings with you when you deplane.

The scheduled departure time for _____ / is (_____ : _____) in the morning (afternoon, evening).

Reboarding will be starting in about _____ minutes.

The boarding will be announced / in the transit area.

Thank you.

Arrival Information : USA

손님 여러분, /
미국 입국에 필요한 서류를 확인해 주시기 바랍니다.

미국 시:민권이나 영:주권 소:지자, / 미국 최:초이민자, / 캐나다 시:민권자를 제외한 /
모:든 분께서는 / 입국 신고서를 작성하셔야 합니다.

세:관 신고서는 / 모:든 분이 작성하셔야 하며, / 가족과 함께 여행하시는 분은 / 세:관
신고서 한 장만 작성하시기 바랍니다.

미화 만 달러 이:상 / 또는 이에 해당하는 외:화를 소:지하시거나, / 과:일이나,
동:식물, 씨앗 또는 음식물을 갖고 계:신 분은 / 세:관 신고서에 신고하십시오.

(경유노선)
계속해서, / 이 비행기로 _____ 까지 가시는 손님 여러분께 안내말씀 드리겠습니다.
손님 여러분의 안전과 항공기 보안을 위해 / (이곳 공항 당국의 요청에 따라) 모든 짐을
가지고 내리시기 바랍니다.
내리신 후에는, / 저희 지상직원의 안내에 따라 / 통과 카드를 받으신 다음, / 공항
라운지에서 잠시 기다려 주십시오.

이 비행기의 출발시간은 _____ 시 _____ 분 입니다.
약 _____ 분 후에 탑승을 시작할 예정이며, 정확한 시간은 공항에서 공항에서 다시
알려드리겠습니다.
감사합니다.

Landing

Ladies and gentlemen, /

We will be landing shortly.

Please stow your carry-on baggage and return your seat back, / and tray table /
to the upright position.

Also please check / that your seat belt is fastened and discontinue the use of all
electronic devices until the aircraft is parked at the gate.

Thank you for your cooperation.

Landing

손님 여러분, /

저희 비행기는 / 곧 착륙하겠습니다.

꺼내 놓으신 짐들은 / 선반 속과 앞 좌석 밑에 보관해 주시고, / 좌석 등 받이와
테이블을 제자리로 해 주십시오.

또한 좌석벨트를 매셨는지 확인해 주시고, / 지금부터 모든 전자기기의 사용을 삼가시기
바랍니다.

감:사합니다.

Farewell Announcement

Ladies and gentlemen, /

We have landed at _____ International Airport.

The local time (here in _____) is _____ AM/PM.

For your safety, please keep your seat belt fastened until the captain turns off
the seat belt sign.

Also, refrain from using your mobile phone / until you deplane.

When opening the overhead bins, / please be careful as the contents may fall out.

Before leaving the aircraft, / please check that there're no items left in your seat pocket / or under your seat.

Please take all carry-on baggage with you / when you deplane.

On behalf of the entire crew, / we've enjoyed serving you today / and we hope to see you soon.

Thank you.

Farewell Announcement

손님 여러분,
저희 비행기는 _____ 공항에 도:착 했습니다.

이곳 _____ 의 현:재 시각은 / _____ 월 _____ 일 오:전(오:후) _____ 시 _____ 분 입니다.

안전을 위해 / 좌:석벨트 착용 표시등이 꺼질 때까지 / 좌:석에서 잠:시만 기다려 주시기 바랍니다.
휴대전:화는 / 비행기에서 내리신 후:, / 사:용해 주십시오.
내리실 때는 / 잊으신 물건이 없:는지 / 좌:석 주변을 확인하시고, / 선반을 여:실 때는 / 안에 있는 물건이 떨어지지 않도록 / 유의(이)해 주시기 바랍니다.

오늘 / 탑승해 주신 손님 여러분께 / 감:사드리며, / 여러분을 기내에서 다시 뵙게 되기를 /진:심으로 기원합니다.

감사합니다.

▶ American Culture 5

문을 열고 닫을 때

· 미국인들은 문을 열고 닫을 때 뒤에 오는 사람을 배려해서 문을 잡고 기다리는 모습을 종종 볼 수 있습니다. 우리나라에서는 뒤에 오는 사람을 위해 문을 잡고 기다리는 모습은 보기 쉽지 않은데 반해서 미국인들은 상대방을 배려해서 문을 잡아주는 것이 예의라고 생각한답니다.

▶ Grammar Note 5: 미래시제(Future Tense)

영어에서 '미래'를 나타내는 몇 가지 방법이 있습니다.

1. Be going to나 Will은 예언이나 미래에 대한 추측을 할 때 사용합니다.
   예 · I am going to check out at 11 o' clock.
   · I will take the shuttle bus.

2. 현재진행형(주어 + be동사 + 본 동사의 ing)은 이미 약속된 미래의 계획을 표현하고자 할 때 사용합니다.
   예 · I am flying to New York tomorrow. I have a ticket.

3. 미래의 계획, 시간표, 프로그램 등을 말할 때, 현재시제를 사용해서 미래를 표현 할 수 있습니다. 주로 사용되는 동사로는 leave, start, end, begin, open, close 등이 있습니다.
   예 · The shop opens at 10:00 A.M.
   · The bus leaves at 3:00 P.M.

   주의 be going to + 동사원형 / will+동사원형 임을 주의 하세요.

참고문헌

- 펼치면항공영어가 보인다(2005), 임주환·차석빈, 백산출판사
- 항공객실서비스론(2006), 김선희·양정미·조영신, 문경출판사
- CABIN SERVICE ENGLISH(2007), 아시아나 항공
- KOREAN AIR IN-FLIGHT ANNOUNCEMENT MANUAL(2003), 대한항공
- INFLIGHT ANNOUNCEMENT MANUAL(2002), 아시아나 항공
- 항공관광영어(2009), 고선희·박정민, 백산출판사
- 항공실무영어(2010), 이동희·권도희, 새로미

저자소개

조영신

동국대학교 대학원 호텔관광경영학 석사
동국대학교 대학원 호텔관광경영학 박사
전) 아시아나 항공 캐빈승무원
전) 방송통신대학교 관광학과 전임강사
전) 중부대학교 항공서비스학과 겸임교수
전) 두원공과대학교 항공서비스과 교수
현) 서울신학대학교 관광경영학과 교수

이승현

경희대학교 관광대학원 관광경영학과 석사
세종대학교 대학원 호텔관광경영학과 박사
전) (주)아시아나 항공 캐빈승무원
전) 케세이퍼시픽 항공 객실승무원
전) 동주대학 항공운항과 초빙교수
전) 한국관광대학 항공서비스과 겸임교수
전) 대림대학 호텔조리외식계열, 백석문화대학 영어학부, 일본어학부 및 관광학부, 백석예술대학
　　항공서비스과 출강
현) 캐나다 유학 중

홍순남

단국대학교 관광호텔경영학 석사
경희대학교 대학원 호텔경영학 전공 박사과정
전) Cathay Pacific Airways 객실승무원
전) 원광보건대학교 항공서비스과 겸임교수
전) 정화예술대학 항공서비스과 외래교수
현) 대림대학 항공서비스과 외래교수
현) 두원공과대학 항공서비스과 강의전담 교수
현) 한국CS코칭개발원 부원장

Essential Airline Service English

2014년 1월 15일 초판1쇄 인쇄
2018년 2월 15일 수정2쇄 발행

저　자　조영신·이승현·홍순남
펴낸이　임순재
펴낸곳　**한올출판사**

　　　　등록 제11-403호
　　　　| 1 | 2 | 1 |-| 8 | 4 | 9 |
주　　　소　서울시 마포구 성산동 133-3 한올빌딩 3층
전　　　화　(02)376-4298(대표)
팩　　　스　(02)302-8073
홈 페 이 지　www.hanol.co.kr
e-메 일　hanol@hanol.co.kr
정　　　가　16,000원

▫ ISBN 978-89-98636-59-3